W9-ADZ-011

This book was purchased with funds provided

from the

TEXAS BOOK FESTIVAL GRANT

awarded to

Howard County Library

Terrorism

by Debra A. Miller

LUCENT BOOKS

A part of Gale, Cengage Learning

Detroit • New York • San Francisco • New Haven, Conn • Waterville, Maine • London

HOWARD COUNTY LIBRARY
BIG SPRING, TEXAS

GALE
CENGAGE Learning™

© 2008 Gale, Cengage Learning

ALL RIGHTS RESERVED. No part of this work covered by the copyright hereon may be reproduced, transmitted, stored, or used in any form or by any means graphic, electronic, or mechanical, including but not limited to photocopying, recording, scanning, digitizing, taping, Web distribution, information networks, or information storage and retrieval systems, except as permitted under Section 107 or 108 of the 1976 United States Copyright Act, without the prior written permission of the publisher.

Every effort has been made to trace the owners of copyrighted material.

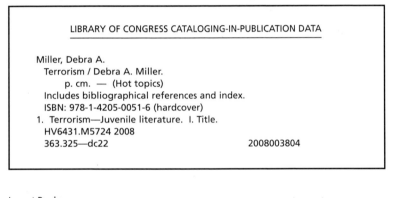

LIBRARY OF CONGRESS CATALOGING-IN-PUBLICATION DATA

Miller, Debra A.
    Terrorism / Debra A. Miller.
        p. cm. — (Hot topics)
    Includes bibliographical references and index.
    ISBN: 978-1-4205-0051-6 (hardcover)
    1. Terrorism—Juvenile literature. I. Title.
    HV6431.M5724 2008
    363.325—dc22   2008003804

Lucent Books
27500 Drake Rd.
Farmington Hills, MI 48331

ISBN-13: 978-1-4205-0051-6
ISBN-10: 1-4205-0051-1

Printed in the United States of America
1 2 3 4 5 6 7 12 11 10 09 08

CONTENTS

FOREWORD

Young people today are bombarded with information. Aside from traditional sources such as newspapers, television, and the radio, they are inundated with a nearly continuous stream of data from electronic media. They send and receive e-mails and instant messages, read and write online "blogs," participate in chat rooms and forums, and surf the Web for hours. This trend is likely to continue. As Patricia Senn Breivik, the former dean of university libraries at Wayne State University in Detroit, has stated, "Information overload will only increase in the future. By 2020, for example, the available body of information is expected to double every 73 days! How will these students find the information they need in this coming tidal wave of information?"

Ironically, this overabundance of information can actually impede efforts to understand complex issues. Whether the topic is abortion, the death penalty, gay rights, or obesity, the deluge of fact and opinion that floods the print and electronic media is overwhelming. The news media report the results of polls and studies that contradict one another. Cable news shows, talk radio programs, and newspaper editorials promote narrow viewpoints and omit facts that challenge their own political biases. The World Wide Web is an electronic minefield where legitimate scholars compete with the postings of ordinary citizens who may or may not be well informed or capable of reasoned argument. At times, strongly worded testimonials and opinion pieces both in print and electronic media are presented as factual accounts.

Conflicting quotes and statistics can confuse even the most diligent researchers. A good example of this is the question of whether or not the death penalty deters crime. For instance, one study found that murders decreased by nearly one-third when the death penalty was reinstated in New York in 1995.

Death penalty supporters cite this finding to support their argument that the existence of the death penalty deters criminals from committing murder. However, another study found that states without the death penalty have murder rates below the national average. This study is cited by opponents of capital punishment, who reject the claim that the death penalty deters murder. Students need context and clear, informed discussion if they are to think critically and make informed decisions.

The Hot Topics series is designed to help young people wade through the glut of fact, opinion, and rhetoric so that they can think critically about controversial issues. Only by reading and thinking critically will they be able to formulate a viewpoint that is not simply the parroted views of others. Each volume of the series focuses on one of today's most pressing social issues and provides a balanced overview of the topic. Carefully crafted narrative, fully documented primary and secondary source quotes, informative sidebars, and study questions all provide excellent starting points for research and discussion. Full-color photographs and charts enhance all volumes in the series. With its many useful features, the Hot Topics series is a valuable resource for young people struggling to understand the pressing issues of the modern era.

INTRODUCTION

THE NEW
U.S. ENEMY

For more than four decades, from the end of World War II in 1945 to the collapse of the Soviet Union in 1991, the United States and the Soviets were engaged in the Cold War—a political conflict between two superpowers and two ideologies (democracy and communism) that threatened at any moment to break into nuclear war. During this period, U.S. national security policy was consumed with maintaining military equality with the Soviets and countering Soviet influence in various parts of the world. This effort cost American taxpayers hundreds of billions of dollars in defense spending and aid to other nations who opposed communism and the Soviet Union. When the Soviet Union collapsed from internal economic and political problems in 1991, the Soviet military threat disappeared and the United States became the world's only remaining superpower. For a few years during the 1990s, ordinary Americans and U.S. policy makers could finally relax, since this extended military and psychological threat was gone. The September 11, 2001, terrorist attacks on the United States, however, marked the beginning of a new era. U.S. president George W. Bush responded to the attacks by declaring a war on terrorism, and many political observers say terrorism has now replaced the Cold War as the United States' main foreign and domestic focus.

In 2006, for example, in a speech at the U.S. military academy at West Point, President Bush himself compared his war on terrorism to the Cold War and promised that the United States will show the same resolve against terrorists as it did against the Soviets. Bush stated:

Like the Cold War, our enemies believe that the innocent can be murdered to serve a political vision. . . . Like the Cold War, they're seeking weapons of mass murder that will allow them to deliver catastrophic destruction to our country. . . . If our enemies succeed in acquiring such weapons, they will not hesitate to use them, which means they would pose a threat to America as great as the Soviet Union.[1]

Not surprisingly, like the Cold War, Bush's war on terrorism comes with a huge cost—measured in hundreds of billions spent on the wars in Afghanistan and Iraq as well as rising counterterrorism and homeland security budgets.

U.S. president George W. Bush compared the war on terrorism to the Cold War, which pitted the United States against the Soviet Union from 1945 until 1991.

The terrorist enemies President Bush refers to are Islamic extremist groups that want the United States to leave the Middle East so that Islamic rule can be instituted throughout the region. The main anti-U.S. terrorist threat is al Qaeda—the group that claimed responsibility for September 11 and previous terrorist attacks against the United States. Although al Qaeda has not carried out another attack within the United States since 9/11, it has grown into a global terrorist network that has con-

Islamic extremist groups want the United States to leave the Middle East so that Islamic rule can be instituted throughout the region.

tinued to attack dozens of other western targets, including U.S. soldiers and military barracks and civilian tourist sites frequented by Americans. Since 2001, for example, groups with connections to al Qaeda have mounted successful suicide attacks in Indonesia, Kenya, Pakistan, Morocco, Turkey, Saudi Arabia, Spain, Britain, Jordan, and Iraq. Since the U.S. invasion in 2003, Iraq has become the new center of Islamist terrorism. Al Qaeda–affiliated fighters there conduct attacks daily against U.S. forces and Iraqi civilians.

Experts expect Islamic terrorism to continue to flourish in the future. Factors such as the development of new weapons and communications technologies will increase terrorists' capabilities. The Internet, for example, has been readily exploited by al Qaeda and has allowed it to spread its violent message and tactics across the globe. Weapons of mass destruction (WMD)—including biological, chemical, or nuclear weapons —are an even bigger concern. Terrorist groups are known to be interested in acquiring such weapons, and many experts predict that the result could be catastrophic suicide attacks in the future. It is this rising threat that the Bush administration believes requires a counterterrorism effort equal to the U.S. Cold War offensive.

Some commentators, however, downplay the significance of the terrorist threat and say it should not define American foreign policy the way the Cold War did. Critics argue that terrorism is a tactic, not an ideology like communism, and declaring war against a tactic makes no sense. In addition, commentators note that terrorism, unlike the Cold War, does not involve a conflict with another nation or group of nations that pose a military threat to the United States. Terrorism, these critics say, is simply a type of sensational violence used by relatively weak extremist groups to attract media publicity and influence government policy—essentially a nonmilitary, psychological/ideological threat. In fact, experts say terrorism does not pose a serious physical risk to most Americans; the chances of being harmed by a terrorist attack within the United States, now or in the future, are very low. Terrorists thus may not be an enemy worthy of a total commitment of the nation's military forces and energies. As retired diplomat Ronald Spiers has put it, "Relying principally on military means [to fight terrorism] is like trying to eliminate a cloud of mosquitoes with a machine gun."[2] Moreover, many observers think that exaggerating the terrorist threat and stoking public fears may actually aid the terrorists' cause.

Whether the war on terror will continue to be pursued with the same means and priority as the Cold War struggle may depend on a number of factors. Another high-casualty terrorist attack in the United States could increase public fears and help maintain the war on terror. On the other hand, public dissatisfaction with the war in Iraq, a new foreign policy crisis, or political changes brought by the 2008 presidential election could move the focus away from a "war" on terror and result in more emphasis on nonmilitary antiterror strategies. Either way, experts say today's trend of Islamic terrorism will likely continue unless terrorists' extremist views lose favor within the Muslim world.

DEFINING TERRORISM

There is no single definition of terrorism agreed upon by experts or political leaders. The difficulty in defining terrorism arises, in part, because throughout history there have been many different brands of terror. Acts of terror have included everything from revolutionary struggles against government oppression, to campaigns fought for land or political independence, to acts of genocide committed by governments themselves. In the early 2000s, terrorism inspired by religious fanaticism has taken a deadly new turn, toward large-scale acts of violence against innocent civilians. All of these examples of violence have been classified as terrorism by those who study the subject.

Various Definitions of "Terrorism"

American historian and well-known terrorism expert Walter Laqueur has counted more than a hundred different contemporary definitions of terrorism. Frequently, the definition depends on one's political goals and objectives, and one's enemies are often labeled terrorists. Governments facing attacks by rebel groups waging unconventional warfare, for example, typically call these groups terrorists as a way to make the rebel group's political demands seem less legitimate. Conversely, viewed from the standpoint of some so-called terrorist groups, governments themselves sometimes appear to be engaged in state-sponsored violence and discrimination against certain populations that could be classified as terrorism. As Laqueur writes, "Perhaps the only characteristic generally agreed upon is that terrorism always involves violence or the threat of violence."[3]

Confessions of a Terrorist

Walid Shoebat is a Palestinian who was once a member of the Palestinian Liberation Organization (PLO), a Palestinian group that has conducted acts of terrorism against Israel. He was taught to hate Jews and admits to committing acts of violence against Israelis, and to spending time in an Israeli prison. Shoebat, however, moved to the United States, renounced terrorism, and in 2005 published a book titled *Why I Left Jihad*. In the book, Shoebat explains jihadism, stating:

> It is no different from the Nazis throwing human beings into ovens. We are witnessing the rise of terror, all over the world, no different from what happened in Nazi Germany. . . . No one was safe then; no one is safe now. . . . With Islamism, only those who adhere to militant, radical fundamentalism are safe; the rest of the world are infidels who must be converted or destroyed. . . . The Jews are not their only target. . . . The rest of you are infidels, too: Koreans, Japanese, Britons, anyone —even other Muslims who don't adhere to this cult of violence. The motto is "Islam to the world." The earth, they claim, belongs to "Allah and His prophet."

Walid Shoebat, *Why I Left Jihad*. United States: Top Executive Media, 2005, pp. 14–15.

In the United States, the government employs numerous definitions for terrorism. The U.S. Department of Defense definition is: "The unlawful use of—or threatened use of—force or violence against individuals or property to coerce or intimidate governments or societies, often to achieve political, religious, or ideological objectives."[4] The U.S. Central Intelligence Agency (CIA), on the other hand, operates under another definition of terrorism: "Premeditated, politically motivated violence perpetrated against noncombatant targets by subnational [not part of a national government] groups or clandestine [secret] agents, usually intended to influence an audience."[5] However, another agency in the U.S. intelligence network—the U.S. National Counterterrorism Center (NCTC), part of the newly created Office of the Director of National Intelligence—employs a slightly different description of terrorist acts: "Premeditated; perpetrated by a subnational or clandestine agent; politically motivated, potentially including religious, philosophical, or culturally symbolic motivations; violent; and perpetrated against a noncombatant target."[6] The U.S. State Department, meanwhile, considers international terrorism to be "terrorism conducted with the support of a foreign government or organization and/or directed against foreign nationals, institutions or governments."[7] The "National Security Strategy of the United States of America," issued by the White House, defines terrorism simply as: "Premeditated, politically motivated violence against innocents."[8]

The United States also defines terrorism as a domestic crime. Under the newly passed Patriot Act, domestic terrorism is defined as:

> Activities that (A) involve acts dangerous to human life that are a violation of the criminal laws of the U.S. or of any state; (B) appear to be intended—(i) to intimidate or coerce a civilian population, (ii) to influence the policy of a government by intimidation or coercion, or (iii) to affect the conduct of a government by mass destruction, assassination, or kidnapping, and (C) occur primarily within the territorial jurisdiction of the U.S.[9]

"I KNOW IT WHEN I SEE IT"

"The most accurate definition of terrorism may be the famous [former U.S. Supreme Court Justice] Potter Stewart standard of obscenity: 'I know it when I see it.'" —Michael Kinsley, an American political journalist and television commentator.

Michael Kinsley, "Defining Terrorism: It's Essential. It's Also Impossible," *Slate*, October 5, 2001. www.slate.com/id/116697.

The main domestic law enforcement agency, the Federal Bureau of Investigation (FBI), however, uses a different definition: "The unlawful use of force and violence against persons or property to intimidate or coerce a government, the civilian population, or any segment thereof, in furtherance of political or social objectives."[10]

The global community of nations has not agreed on a definition either. Members of the United Nations (UN) have not been able to formally adopt a definition, although several proposals have been offered. An early proposal in 1937, for example, contained this definition: "All criminal acts directed against a State and intended or calculated to create a state of terror in the minds of particular persons or a group of persons or the general public."[11] A resolution proposed in 1999 referred to terrorism as "criminal acts intended or calculated to provoke a state of terror in the general public, a group of persons or particular persons for political purposes."[12] Academics at the UN, meanwhile, often rely upon a much wordier definition:

TERRORISTS ARE NOT FREEDOM FIGHTERS

"The fact that terrorists may claim to be freedom fighters does not mean that we should concede the point to them." —Louise Richardson, executive dean of the Radcliffe Institute for Advanced Study, a senior lecturer in government at Harvard University, and a lecturer on law at Harvard Law School.

Louise Richardson, *What Terrorists Want.* New York: Random House, 2006, p. 7.

An anxiety-inspiring method of repeated violent action, employed by (semi) clandestine individual, group or state actors, for idiosyncratic, criminal or political reasons, whereby—in contrast to assassination—the direct targets of violence are not the main targets. The immediate human victims of violence are generally chosen randomly (targets of opportunity) or selectively (representative or symbolic targets) from a target population, and serve as message generators. Threat- and violence-based communication processes between terrorist (organization), (imperiled) victims, and main targets are used to manipulate the main target (audience(s)), turning it into a target of terror, a target of demands, or a target of attention, depending on whether intimidation, coercion, or propaganda is primarily sought.[13]

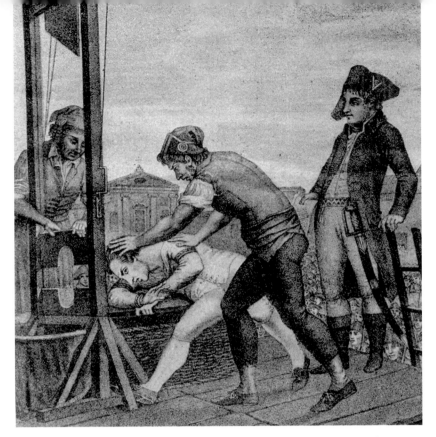

Maximilien Robespierre was beheaded in 1794 for his actions in support of a new government during the French Revolution.

In 2005, yet another definition was used by a UN panel—any act "intended to cause death or serious bodily harm to civilians or non-combatants with the purpose of intimidating a population or compelling a government or an international organization to do or abstain from doing any act."[14]

These various definitions differ in many respects, but there are also similarities. Most definitions, for example, share the idea that terrorism involves extremely violent acts intended to create fear or terror, often for an ideological, religious, or political purpose. Most terrorism experts also note that terrorists typically use unconventional methods of warfare, and often (but not always) direct their violence against innocent civilians or noncombatants rather than the government or entity that they seek to influence.

Experts say a more uniform definition of terrorism would help nations prosecute terrorist actions within their borders and gain cooperation from other nations to fight terrorism on a global scale. As long as nations cannot agree on the definition, each country will employ a different legal standard and nations will have trouble convincing other nations to extradite, or hand over, persons who have committed terrorist acts for prosecution and punishment.

Revolutionary Terrorism

Commentators seem to agree that the reason terrorism is so difficult to define is because it has been applied to many different types of actors and to a variety of motives and tactics. As terrorism expert Bruce Hoffman puts it, "The most compelling reason [terrorism is hard to define] is because the meaning of the term has changed so frequently over the past two hundred years."[15]

The term "terrorism" was first used during the 1789 French Revolution, and originally it had a positive meaning. A peasant rebellion in France against King Louis XVI ushered in a new revolutionary government committed to economic and democratic reforms. The leader of this revolution, Maximilien Robespierre, launched a reign of terror—a campaign that killed between eighteen thousand and forty thousand people who opposed or were considered a threat to the new government. Executions were conducted publicly using the guillotine, a machine that quickly and efficiently beheaded those condemned as traitors. In this context, terrorism was a tool used to protect the state. As Robespierre explained at the time, "Terror is nothing but justice, prompt, severe and inflexible."[16]

Violent tactics were again used during the Russian Revolution in the late nineteenth century. A political philosophy known as anarchism arose in Europe and Russia advocating the use of violence to overthrow unjust governments. Using a deadly new technology—explosive bombs—a group called the People's Will assassinated Czar Alexander II in 1881 and unleashed a wave of assassinations and bombings throughout the country. Historians say the violent protests eventually helped to weaken the cruel czarist system of government in Russia.

The acts of revolutionary terrorism in Russia inspired similar strikes against heads of state and other government targets in countries around the globe. In the 1880s and 1890s, for example, political discontent similar to the anticzarist sentiment in Russia grew in various parts of the decaying Ottoman Empire— a vast, Turkish-ruled dynasty that covered parts of Asia, Africa, and Europe. In addition, American presidents James Garfield and William McKinley were assassinated during this period, along with two prime ministers of Japan, leaders in India, a French president, an Austrian empress, and a king of Italy.

The most famous act of terrorism during this time, however, occurred in Bosnia and helped to launch World War I. A group of Bosnian Serb intellectuals and students known as Young Bosnia rose up against the governing Habsburg monarchy, which was centered in Austria and ruled much of Europe. On June 28, 1914, one member of this group, Gavrilo Princip, assassinated the Habsburg archduke Franz Ferdinand. The goal

Assassin Gavrilo Princip, right, is captured after killing Austrian Archduke Franz Ferdinand in 1914. This act of terrorism led to the launch of World War I.

was to break off the southern part of the Austrian Empire to join with neighboring Serbia to form an independent state comprised of Bosnia, Serbia, and other southern Slav lands. The plan backfired, however, when the Austrian government declared war on Serbia and the growing conflict pulled most of the big powers of Europe into World War I.

State Terrorism

The next wave of violence that has been labeled as terrorism by historians involves repression and abuse of power by established governments. This type of terrorism is frequently called state terror. The Russian Revolution, for example, led to the creation of an authoritarian Communist state and to the rise of Joseph Stalin, a leader who implemented a massive campaign of repression and state-run terror designed to eliminate all threats to his rule. During the 1930s, Stalin, through his Great Purge

This map outlines a few leaders who used terrorist tactics against their own people to help their rise to power in the twentieth century.

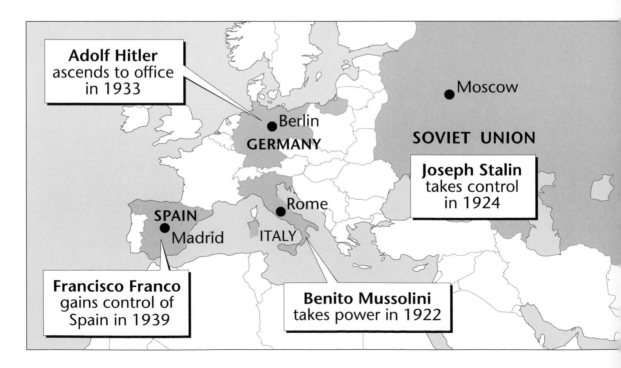

Adolf Hitler ascends to office in 1933

Moscow

Berlin
GERMANY

SOVIET UNION

Joseph Stalin takes control in 1924

Rome

SPAIN
Madrid   ITALY

Francisco Franco gains control of Spain in 1939

Benito Mussolini takes power in 1922

campaign, arrested more than 1.2 million people. About 600,000 ultimately died from torture, execution, or in Russia's inhumane prison system, the gulag.

About the same time, in the 1930s and 1940s, another dictator, Adolf Hitler of Germany, implemented a horrific program to exterminate Jews and others considered to be unworthy of German citizenship. This campaign of state genocide, later known as the Holocaust, is estimated to have killed as many as 11 million people, including about 6 million Jews. State terror was also used by one of Hitler's close allies, Benito Mussolini, a fascist dictator who ruled Italy from 1922 until 1943. Using armed militia known as the "Blackshirts," and later a secret police force, Mussolini eliminated all resistance to his regime and strongly supported Germany's anti-Semitic policies.

Since then, other nations have also used terror to suppress their citizens. In the 1960s and the 1970s, for example, Indonesian troops killed, raped, and brutalized thousands of civilians in West Papua and East Timor—regions that were seeking independence from the Indonesian government. Also

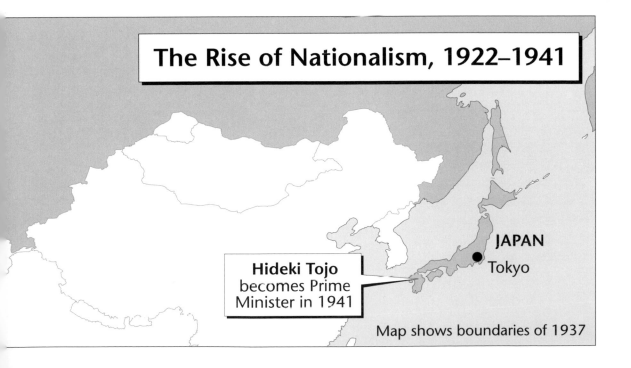

The Rise of Nationalism, 1922–1941

Hideki Tojo becomes Prime Minister in 1941

JAPAN
Tokyo

Map shows boundaries of 1937

in the 1970s, the Khmer Rouge regime in Cambodia, led by Pol Pot, became infamous for beating, starving, or torturing an estimated million and a half Cambodians as part of a plan to force the population to work in state labor camps and create a Communist economy.

"Terrorists" vs. "Freedom Fighters"

Following the end of World War II in 1945, the term terrorism was again applied to revolutionary, antigovernment movements —many of them rebellions against European colonial rule. Governments typically called rebel groups terrorists as a form of propaganda, in order to portray them in a bad light and discount their demands. Rebel groups, on the other hand, saw themselves as freedom fighters for the cause of political independence or political change. Most groups used the conventional weapons of the age, including machine guns and explosives, and although civilians were sometimes inadvertently killed, they targeted mostly government officers and soldiers, causing relatively limited casualties. Rebels justified their use of violence as necessary to acquire freedom and independence from governments that oppressed them.

TERRORIST ACTS GET ATTENTION

"Terrorism has been with us for centuries, and it has always attracted inordinate attention because of its dramatic character and its sudden, often wholly unexpected, occurrence." —Walter Laqueur, an American historian, political commentator, and former cochairman of the International Research Council, a project of the Center for Strategic and International Studies.

Walter Laqueur, *The New Terrorism: Fanaticism and the Arms of Mass Destruction.* New York: Oxford University Press, 1999, pp. 3–4.

During the 1940s, for example, Jews who escaped Nazi and European persecution by immigrating to Palestine formed groups, such as the Stern Gang and the Irgun, dedicated to forcing the end of British rule in the region and creating an independent Jew-

The Irish Republican Army (IRA) conducted numerous bombings and assassinations to protest British rule in Northern Ireland.

ish state. These groups relentlessly attacked British military offices and soldiers stationed in Palestine, and they were repeatedly condemned by government leaders as terrorists. However, these attacks resulted in the creation of the nation of Israel in 1948, and later two former Jewish terrorist leaders, Yitzhak Shamir and Menachem Begin, were elected as prime ministers of Israel. As Walter Laqueur explains, "These are just two examples of the many cases of guerrilla or terrorist leaders having a second, political career after their fighting days were over."[17]

In the 1950s, a similar anticolonial fight for independence took place in French-controlled Algeria. The Front de Liberation Nationale (FLN), a Muslim resistance group, spearheaded the effort with guerrilla attacks on French government targets, often staged from neighboring countries that protected the FLN. By March 1962, the FLN attacks had worn down the French government, and the two sides signed a cease-fire. Full independence for Algeria followed later that same year, and the FLN became the ruling political party.

Another political rebellion classified as terrorism during this period included the Irish Republican Army's (IRA) guerrilla campaign against British rule in Northern Ireland. An earlier IRA campaign in the 1920s had divided Ireland into two parts—a southern, predominantly Catholic region that was granted independence from Britain, and a northern, mostly Protestant district called Ulster, which remained under British control. However, the IRA, together with many Catholic "republicans" in Ulster, continued to push for a united Ireland that would be wholly independent from British rule. Beginning in the late 1960s, the IRA conducted numerous bombing and assassina-

Timothy McVeigh committed the most deadly act of domestic terrorism in U.S. history when he bombed the Alfred Murrah Federal Building in Oklahoma City, Oklahoma, on April 19, 1995.

Ecoterrorism

One form of domestic terrorism is called ecoterrorism. Ecoterrorism is defined by the Federal Bureau of Investigation (FBI) as "the use or threatened use of violence of a criminal nature against innocent victims or property by an environmentally-oriented, subnational group for environmental-political reasons, or aimed at an audience beyond the target, often of a symbolic nature." This term and its definition are somewhat controversial, however, because it includes acts of protest aimed at protecting animals or the environment that are usually limited to destruction of property. In fact, so far no one has been physically injured by acts of ecoterrorism in the United States. One of the largest so-called ecoterrorism groups, for example, is the Animal Liberation Front (ALF), an animal rights group that has been linked with crimes such as breaking into animal laboratories to release the animals and sabotaging whaling ships. ALF's environmental equivalent is the Earth Liberation Front (ELF), an extremist environmental group that carries out acts of arson against construction that it considers to be damaging to the environment. On August 1, 2003, for example, self-identified ELF arsonists burned down a housing complex under construction in San Diego, California, creating losses estimated at $50 million.

James F. Jarboe, domestic terrorism section chief, Counterterrorism Division, FBI, Testimony before the House Resources Committee, Subcommittee on Forests and Forest Health, "The Threat of Eco-Terrorism," February 12, 2002. http://www.fbi.gov/congress/congress02/jarboe021202.htm.

tion attacks. The attacks were aimed primarily at British troops, police officers, prison guards, and judges. After many decades of violence, under a peace accord negotiated in 1998, Northern Ireland was granted self-rule, a parliament was formed, and the IRA agreed to disarm. This accord later unraveled, but in 2007 self-rule was reinstated.

The 1960s brought political terrorism to other regions as well. In Spain, Basque separatists formed the Euskadi ta Askatasuna (ETA) and demanded independence in response to repression by the dictator Francisco Franco. In South Africa, the African National Congress (ANC) and its terrorist arm, Umkhonto we Sizwe (MK, or Spear of the Nation, led by Nelson Mandela), waged terrorist attacks against the racist white government and its system of apartheid using arson, explosives, and sabotage. In Latin America, in countries such as Uruguay, Argentina, Brazil, Colombia, Peru, and Venezuela, leftist radicals organized groups that conducted robberies, kidnappings of government officials, and other tactics to undermine governments viewed as illegitimate and repressive.

The 1960s also saw the beginning of politically motivated Arab terrorism in the Middle East. In 1964, seventeen years after the creation of the Jewish nation of Israel amid Arab lands, the Palestine Liberation Organization (PLO) was founded to free Palestinians from what they believed was unjust Israeli occupation. Following the 1967 Arab-Israeli war, during which Israel expanded into several additional Arab territories, PLO leader Yasser Arafat waged a prolonged, bloody terror campaign against Israel. The PLO received financial support from Arab nations such as Libya, a country led by dictator Muammar Qaddafi, who in the 1970s and 1980s became one of the world's most well-known terrorists. Israel called the Palestinian violence terrorism, but Palestinian terrorists have long viewed themselves as revolutionaries seeking freedom for the Palestinian people. As the late Arafat once explained, "The difference between the revolutionary and the terrorist lies in the reason for which each fights. For whoever stands by a just cause and fights for the freedom and liberation of his land from the invaders, the settlers and the colonists, cannot possibly be called terrorist."[18]

Domestic Terrorism

Terrorism tactics have also been used by U.S. citizens within the United States. In 1892, for example, radical anarchist and naturalized citizen Emma Goldman conspired with a colleague, Alexander Berkman, to bomb Carnegie Steel Company executive Henry Clay Frick in retaliation for the company's shooting of workers during a strike. In the 1960s and 1970s, the U.S. government itself became the target of left-wing domestic terrorism, this time waged by students. The two most prominent groups were the Black Panther Party, which opposed racial discrimination and oppression and took up arms against the police, and the Weather Underground, which primarily bombed government facilities to protest the United States' involvement in the Vietnam War. Similar attacks were conducted in Europe by groups such as the Red Brigades in Italy and the Red Army in Germany—groups that opposed capitalism, imperialism, and colonialism.

The most deadly act of domestic terrorism in U.S. history, however, occurred on April 19, 1995, when gun enthusiast and former Army soldier Timothy McVeigh blew up a U.S. government office building in Oklahoma City, Oklahoma. The massive bombing killed 168 people and injured another 853.

Modern Terrorists

Today, the world continues to produce many different forms of terrorism. Like past revolutionary terrorists, some modern-day actors use terrorist tactics to achieve political independence and other nationalist goals. Since the collapse of the Soviet Union in 1991, for example, an Islamic ethnic group called the Chechens (named after where they are from, the Russian republic of Chechnya) has waged a struggle for independence. Strikes by both the Russian military and the Chechen separatists have killed many civilians, and hostilities continued into the early twenty-first century. Sri Lanka is the site of a similar struggle for political independence. There, the Liberation Tigers of Tamil Eelam (LTTE or "Tamil Tigers") fights to win freedom for a minority ethnic group, the Tamils, from that country's majority ethnic group, the Sinhalese. A twenty-year civil war between the Tamils and the Sinhalese has killed more than sixty-five thousand people, displaced more than 1.5 million others, and has included numerous Tamil suicide attacks—that is, bomb attacks in which the attacker also dies. In fact, experts say the Tamils have conducted more suicide bombings than any other contemporary terrorist group. And in the relatively stable country of Turkey, a group called the Kurdistan Workers Party (PKK) wages a terrorist fight to create an independent socialist Kurdish state of Kurdistan that would cover parts of Turkey, Iraq, Syria, and Iran. Since the PKK's founding in 1974, the conflict has caused thousands of deaths, many of them civilian.

Examples of state terrorism also exist in the modern world. In the early 1990s Bosnian Serbs, together with Slobodan

Milosevic's regime in Serbia, attacked the non-Serb, Muslim population in Bosnia-Herzegovina, an independent republic that once was part of Yugoslavia. Approximately 700,000 people were slaughtered in this campaign, which was euphemistically called "ethnic cleansing." In 1994, yet another genocide campaign was conducted in Rwanda, a small country in east-central Africa made up of two main tribes, Hutus and Tutsis. After a plane carrying the Hutu Rwandan president Juvenal Habyarimana was shot down in April 1994, the presidential guard and other government officials, believing the shooting to be a Tutsi action, sanctioned the killing of an estimated 800,000 Tutsi and politically moderate Hutus over a period of just three months.

A campaign of state-run terror has also developed in the African country of Sudan, after an authoritarian, Islamist-Arab government took power in 1989. Since then, Sudanese armed forces and government-supported Arab militias known as the Janjaweed have attacked the country's black population without mercy. In one region of the country, called Darfur, these attacks

In Sri Lanka the Tamil Tigers, pictured, fight to win freedom for a minority ethnic group, the Tamils.

have killed more than 400,000 people, many thousands have been raped, and whole villages have been destroyed, forcing more than 2 million people to leave the country.

Other modern-day terrorists are linked with drugs and crime. The best example of this phenomenon, called narcoterrorism, is found in the Latin American country of Colombia. The Revolutionary Forces of Colombia (FARC) was founded in 1964 as a socialist, antigovernment group, but since then it has turned to drug trafficking as a way to fund its activities. The group uses drug funds to buy government officials, destabilize the government, and spread corruption throughout the region, but many commentators say the group now is primarily a criminal gang dedicated to enriching its members.

NAMING THE ENEMY

"[Terrorism] is a word . . . that is generally applied to one's enemies and opponents, or to those with whom one disagrees and would otherwise prefer to ignore." —Bruce Hoffman, professor of security studies at Georgetown University's Edmund A. Walsh School of Foreign Service and a recognized expert on terrorism.

Bruce Hoffman, *Inside Terrorism*. New York: Columbia University Press, 1998, p. 31.

By far the most significant terrorism trend in contemporary times, however, is religion-based and centered in the Middle East. Radical Islamists condemn the corruption of Islam by any non-Muslim influences, especially American culture, and seek to create Islamic states in the region. Although this movement is diverse and made up of many different groups and individuals, the world's most notorious radical Islamic group is al Qaeda, the group responsible for the September 11, 2001, World Trade Center massacre. Unlike many past terrorists, al Qaeda plans spectacular suicide attacks that kill as many civilians as possible. Until 9/11, many Americans were largely unaware of terrorism. Those who study the issue, however, know that al Qaeda's terrorism threat is simply the latest, most lethal version of a phenomenon that has existed throughout history.

THE CURRENT THREAT: ISLAMIC TERRORISM

For most Americans, the word "terrorism" immediately evokes an image of a fundamentalist Islamic suicide bomber from the Middle East. This is not surprising because the phenomenon of radical Islamic terrorism is currently responsible for most of the world's terrorist activity, and its main target is the United States and its allies. This brand of terrorism is also called jihadism. Jihad is an Arabic word that means "striving in the way of God," and it is often used to mean trying to be a better person; however, jihad is also used to refer to a war fought in defense of Islam. As terrorism experts Monte Palmer and Princess Palmer explain, "The jihadists are a self-appointed collection of religious fanatics who have launched a holy war, a jihad, against the United States and everything American."[19] This movement began in the 1980s in the Middle East, mushroomed in the new millennium following the U.S. invasion of Iraq, and now has spread across the globe. Defeating these jihadists is the main focus of the U.S. war on terror.

The Rise of Islamic Fundamentalism

Commentators say the link between Islam and modern terrorism is clear. Many recent terrorist attacks, including the September 11, 2001, attacks on the United States, were committed by Muslims (followers of Islam), and some Muslims applaud these attacks and express their support for Osama bin Laden, al Qaeda's founder. However, Islam is one of the world's great religions, and as terrorism expert and author Louise Richardson reports, "Muslims constitute about a fifth of the world's population, form a majority in forty-five countries . . ., and exist in significant and growing numbers in the United States, Europe, and the former Soviet Union."[20] The vast majority of the world's Muslims, both members of the Sunni and the Shia sects of Islam, are moderate in their views and do not support jihadist terrorism. Some Muslims even see this fundamentalist interpretation of Islam as completely against the true teachings of the religion. Those who believe in terrorist jihad are a minority who follow extremist, fundamentalist versions of the Islamic religion.

This map shows the Ottoman Empire, governed according to Islamic law, at the peak of its power in the 1700s. Controlling much of Southeastern Europe, the Middle East, and North Africa, the Ottoman Turks sought to advance the Islamic religion and spread the reach of Islamic rule.

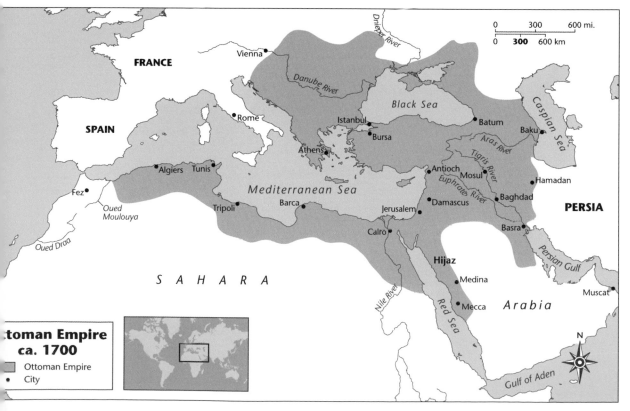

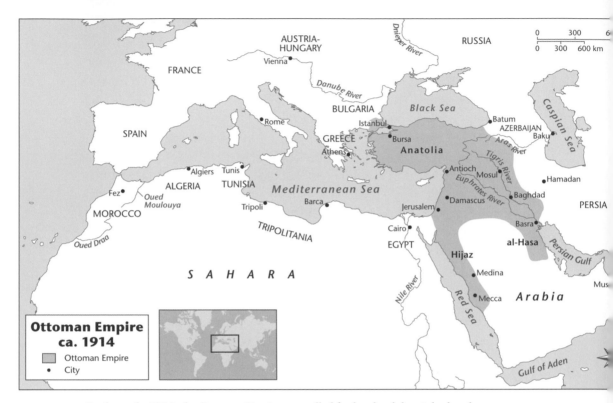

By the early 1900s the Ottoman Empire controlled far less land than it had at the height of its power. At the same time, western nations such as the United States, Britain, and other European countries were becoming world powers.

Some historians trace the beginnings of fundamentalist Islam to the end of the nineteenth century, when the once-great Islamic power, the Ottoman Empire, began to lose influence in the Middle East. First established in the late thirteenth century in the region now known as Turkey, this great dynasty at its height spanned three continents and controlled much of southeastern Europe, the Middle East, and North Africa. The Ottoman Turks were followers of Islam and governed according to Islamic law, called sharia. Although they tolerated other religions, the Turks sought to advance the Islamic religion and spread the reach of Islamic rule. By the early nineteenth century, however, the empire was rapidly collapsing economically, while western powers such as the United States, Britain, and other European countries were industrializing and transforming into world powers. Following World War I, the former Allied Powers (the United States, Britain, Russia, and Italy) saw the Ottoman lands as an opportunity to expand trade and secure a steady supply of oil, which was then becoming the world's main source of energy. The Allied Powers carved up most of the Ottoman Empire into modern countries that they controlled and soon began to dominate much of the Middle East region.

In this new era, Muslim regions that once were ruled by Islamic law were suddenly ruled by secular (nonreligious) political leaders who maintained close ties with western countries and envisioned a modern Arab world built not on religion but on science, trade, and industrialization. Connections with the West and oil wealth brought quick prosperity to some Middle East nations, and many Muslims supported this new direction and saw it as a way to revive Islamic power. Other more conservative Muslims, however, feared that science and western values would destroy core Islamic teachings and weaken Islam. Within both sects of Islam—Sunni and Shia (or Shiites)—a minority of Muslims believed that the solution was a return to the fundamental principles of the Koran, the Islamic holy book, and the teachings of the prophet Muhammad, the founder of Islam.

THREATS TO AMERICA EXAGGERATED

"Although it remains heretical [unpopular] to say so, the evidence so far suggests that . . . the threat presented within the United States by al Qaeda [has been] greatly exaggerated."
—John Mueller, political science professor at Ohio State University and author.

John Mueller, "Is There Still a Terrorist Threat?" *Foreign Affairs*, September/October 2006. www.foreignaffairs.org/20060901facomment85501/john-mueller/is-there-still-a-terrorist-threat.html.

This fundamentalist branch of Islam first arose in three countries: Saudi Arabia, Egypt, and Pakistan. In Saudi Arabia, a primarily Sunni Arab country, it stemmed from the preachings of Muhammad ibn 'Abd al-Wahhab at-Tamimi, an Arab theologian from the eighteenth century. Al-Wahhab, in turn, was influenced by the writings of Ibn Taymiyyah, a Muslim scholar who lived during the thirteenth and fourteenth centuries and who believed that political leaders must strictly follow sharia. This particular brand of fundamentalist Islam became known as Wahhabism and eventually became the accepted religion of Saudi rulers. In 1924, members of the al-Saud family, followers of Wahhabism, conquered Mecca and Medina, two Muslim holy cities, and in 1932 they founded the kingdom of Saudi Arabia. The discovery of oil in the region in 1938, in turn, provided revenues that funded a system of religious schools, newspapers, and other institutions to further spread the Wahhabi theology. The al-Saud family still rules Saudi Arabia and its legitimacy is closely connected to its continuing support for Wahhabism.

The teachings of Ibn Taymiyyah also became the basis for a fundamentalist Sunni Islam sect in Egypt. In 1928 an Egyptian schoolteacher, Hassan al-Bana, founded the Muslim Brotherhood, a religious organization dedicated to promoting a strict interpretation of Islam. As it grew, the group was guided by the writings of Ibn Taymiyyah and later Sayeed Qutb, a leading Muslim thinker who wrote during the 1950s and 1960s. One of Qutb's main arguments was that Muslims must declare a holy war, or jihad, against secular Muslim leaders and reimpose Islamic rule, by force if necessary, throughout the Middle East. Following this creed, the Muslim Brotherhood periodically pushed for Egypt to be governed by sharia, and the group was suspected to be involved in several assassination attempts on secular Arab leaders who failed to implement their demands. Following a humiliating defeat of Egyptian forces by Israel in the 1967 Six Day War, for example, the Muslim Brotherhood insisted that incoming Egyptian president Anwar Sadat establish an Islamic government. This did not happen, however, and four members of a group affiliated with the Brotherhood—the Islamic Jihad—assassinated Sadat in 1981. The Muslim Brotherhood and two other extremist groups—the Islamic Jihad and the Islamic Group—continue to operate in Egypt today.

A third strain of jihadism emerged in Pakistan, a country neighboring India and Asia that has a tradition of Islamic religious schools, many of which adhere to extreme interpretations

Shia vs. Sunni Islam

Centuries ago, the religion of Islam divided into two sects—Shia (or Shiite) and Sunni. The split occurred soon after the death of the prophet Muhammad in 632 over the issue of who would succeed him. Most Muslims at that time wanted the most capable person available to succeed the prophet, but a smaller group insisted that someone from his family should be chosen, such as the prophet's son-in-law Ali. The Sunnis prevailed and chose a successor who was not a family member, but the Shias objected and war broke out, splitting Islam forever into the two separate sects. Today, Shias remain a minority, making up only about 10 to 15 percent of all Muslims, with their population concentrated in Iran, Iraq, and Lebanon. Despite their religious differences, during most of recent history, Sunni and Shia Muslims lived together peacefully in the Arab world. In recent years, however, hostilities have broken out between the two groups due to disputes over political power. This is most evident in Iraq, a predominantly Shia country that was dominated politically by Sunnis until the 2003 U.S. invasion. Today, the two sides fight each other for power in the country.

of Sunni Islam similar to the Wahhabi beliefs in Saudi Arabia. Pakistan also is home to a large religious organization called the Tabligi Jamaat, which zealously advocates fundamentalist Islamic values. In addition, the country has experienced years of political unrest characterized by a struggle between those who want a secular government and those who favor an Islamic, religion-based government. This unrest has further strengthened the country's religious schools and fostered a jihadist movement made up of a number of groups, among them the Harakat ul-Mujahideen (HuM) and the Lashkar-e-Toiba (LT). Many of these groups are centered in Kashmir, a predominantly Muslim region on the Pakistani-Indian border claimed by both countries. From there, militants launch strikes against India, a primarily Hindu country that they view as anti-Muslim.

The Roots of Jihadist Terrorism

Despite their agitation within their own countries, extremist Islamic groups remained on the sidelines of mainstream Muslim life for many years. In recent decades, however, fundamentalist Islam has exploded in popularity, and experts say it has inspired today's phenomenon of global Islamic terrorism. Many commentators believe that this growth of radical Islam and jihadist terrorism can be attributed to three contemporary political events.

The first of these events occurred in 1979, when a fundamentalist Islamic revolution led by the Ayatollah Khomeini overthrew the pro-western shah (or king) of Iran, Mohammad Reza Pahlavi. Khomeini, a Shia religious leader, then openly an-

In 1979 the Ayatollah Khomeini, center, led an Islamic revolution in Iran by overthrowing the shah of Iran.

nounced his intention to spread his religious revolution throughout the world, and Iran soon became known as a sponsor of terrorism. In November 1979, for example, Iranian students seized the American embassy in Tehran, Iran's capital city, to protest the admission of the shah of Iran into the United States for medical treatment. Fifty-two American hostages were held for a total of 444 days, until the United States was forced to negotiate their release in January 1981. U.S. president Jimmy Carter proved unable to secure the hostages' quick release and was widely perceived as being weak on terrorism. He failed to win reelection at home, and many observers say his actions caused radical Islamist elements to believe that the United States might be vulnerable to terrorist violence.

AL QAEDA WANTS THE UNITED STATES OUT OF THE MIDDLE EAST

"[Osama bin Laden] has no interest in attempting to convert Americans or others; he wants the West to remove itself from the Muslim world, broadly defined, so that it can return to the days of the caliphate and the law of Sharia." —Louise Richardson, executive dean of the Radcliffe Institute for Advanced Study, a senior lecturer in government at Harvard University, and a lecturer on law at Harvard Law School.

Louise Richardson, *What Terrorists Want.* New York: Random House, 2006, p. 63.

The second event crucial to the spread of radical Islam was the 1982 war in Lebanon that began when Israeli troops occupied southern Lebanon to protect Israel's northern border from Palestinian guerrilla attacks. PLO forces at that time were based in Beirut, the Lebanese capital. In response to the Israeli action, an Iranian-supported terrorist Islamic group called Hezbollah (or Party of God) was formed to oust Israel from that country. Hezbollah soon became famous for three types of terrorism: airplane hijackings, kidnappings of western citizens, and suicide bombings. After suicide car bomb strikes on American and French soldiers stationed in Beirut as peacekeepers, for example,

Hezbollah was successful in forcing the United States, other foreign troops, and later Israel to withdraw from Lebanon. Although then-U.S. president Ronald Reagan was elected to succeed President Carter because he projected an image of strength, he, too, withdrew instead of engaging Muslim terrorists. As Richardson puts it, "The [U.S.] withdrawal from Lebanon provided example number two of how a superpower can be humiliated by a determined and much weaker adversary prepared to use violence against it."[21]

AL QAEDA'S ROLE IN IRAQ IS MINOR

"Al-Qaeda in Iraq is a microscopic terrorist organization."
—Malcolm Nance, a twenty-six-year veteran of the U.S. intelligence community, an expert on the Iraq insurgency, and the author of the 2007 book *The Terrorists of Iraq: Inside the Strategy and Tactics of the Iraq Insurgency*.

Quoted in Andrew Tilghman, "The Myth of AQI," *Washington Monthly*, October 2007. www.washingtonmonthly.com/features/2007/0710.tilghman.html.

Yet a third event that helped to boost Islamic terrorism was a jihadist war against the Soviet Union in Afghanistan. The Soviets invaded Afghanistan in 1979 in an effort to suppress the spread of Iranian Islamic fundamentalism to the nearby Soviet republics of Uzbekistan, Tajikistan, and Turkmenistan. The Soviet presence, however, attracted an army of Islamic militants, called mujahideen, from across the Muslim world—all of them dedicated to fundamentalist Islam. A large number of the mujahideen were funded and trained by Sunni Muslim Osama bin Laden, who later founded the al Qaeda terrorist group. For ten years, these Muslim fighters fought the powerful Soviet army, in the process acquiring valuable warfare experience and cementing connections between various Muslim jihadist groups. The mujahideen also learned to use sophisticated weapons, many of which were actually supplied by the United States to help defeat the Soviet Union because it was an enemy of the United States at the time. The Soviets were forced to withdraw in 1989,

Members of the Islamic terrorist organization Hezbollah gather at an anti-American demonstration in Beirut, Lebanon, in 1987.

and the lesson learned by Islamic fundamentalists was that they could defeat a superpower militarily. Monte Palmer and Princess Palmer explain: "The jihadists emerged from the war in Afghanistan with an exhilarating sense of victory and an unshakable faith in their ability to reclaim the Islamic world in the name of Allah."[22]

Altogether, these political events showed Muslim militants that they could stand up to world superpowers such as the Soviet Union and the United States. Bin Laden became a role model for young, radicalized Muslims, and Islamic fundamentalism began to spread like wildfire throughout the Muslim world.

The Beginning of Jihad

After the Afghanistan war, Osama bin Laden returned to Saudi Arabia to a hero's welcome. Even the Saudi royal family celebrated Bin Laden's victory over the Soviets. Relations between Bin Laden and Saudi leaders broke down, however, following Iraq's invasion of neighboring Kuwait in 1990. Fearful that Iraq would invade Saudi Arabia next, the Saudis turned to the

Contemporary Jihadist Groups

Al Qaeda is not the only jihadist group active today. During the 1990s groups desiring Islamic rule formed throughout the Muslim world. One radical Muslim group—the Armed Islamic Group (GIA)—emerged in Algeria, after the secular Muslim government called the National Liberation Front (FLN) failed to bring prosperity to the country. In 1991, after the government voided the election of a fundamentalist Islamic opposition party, the GIA declared a jihad, or holy war, against the Algerian government and began a campaign of terrorist strikes against foreigners and other civilian targets. The civil war continued until 2002, when most of the terrorists had been killed or taken advantage of amnesty offers from the government. Two other fundamentalist Islamic groups—Hamas and the Islamic Jihad—began to challenge the more secular PLO (also called Fatah) for leadership of the Palestinians in their struggle to defeat Israel and form a Palestinian state. Yet another fundamentalist Islamic group, Hezbollah, operates in Lebanon and has close ties with Shia Muslim leaders in Iran. In addition, al Qaeda has inspired countless other contemporary jihadist groups around the globe, some of which defer to al Qaeda's leadership and some that operate independently.

United States for protection and permitted U.S. troops to be stationed on Saudi soil, a region that Muslims consider to be the heart of the Islamic world. The Saudi royals reportedly refused an offer from Bin Laden to protect the country with his army of mujahideen fighters.

Following this rejection in Saudi Arabia, Bin Laden moved his operations to Sudan, a Muslim country in Africa that borders Egypt. In 1989 a militant Islamic group called the National Islamic Front overthrew the elected government of Prime Minister Sadiq al-Mahdi in a military coup, turning the country into a haven for terrorists. Once there, Bin Laden joined forces with a Muslim cleric named Hassan Abdalla al-Turabi, who already had contacts with Shia Islamic leader Ayatollah Khomeini in Iran and who, like Bin Laden, wanted to form a global Islamic organization to re-impose Islamic rule in the Middle East. Although there was an underlying tension between Shia and

Sunni factions, the three leaders reportedly began working together in 1991 to channel information, training, and other support to various jihadist groups in the region.

Jihadist Attacks on the United States

The global jihadist network became stronger in the 1990s and began launching attacks on U.S. targets. In the first significant attack, on February 26, 1993, a van loaded with explosives was detonated in the World Trade Center in New York City, killing six people and injuring more than one thousand. A second attack happened in Somalia in October 1993. Eighteen U.S. servicemen who were part of a humanitarian mission to that country were killed in a bloody ambush by jihadists. The United States withdrew its forces from Somalia shortly after the attack, and as Monte Palmer and Princess Palmer explain, this "reinforced the jihadist conviction that the United States would withdraw from a country rather than take casualties."[23]

In November 1995, the attacks against the United States continued with the bombing of a Saudi National Guard barracks in

The bombing of the U.S. embassy in Nairobi, Kenya, in August 1998, was one of the first terrorist actions undertaken by the newly formed jihadist network called al Qaeda.

Riyadh, Saudi Arabia. Five American military trainers staying in the barracks were killed, and many others were wounded. A second attack occurred a few months later, when bombs were detonated in the Khobar Towers, a U.S. Marine facility in Dhahran, Saudi Arabia, killing 241 Americans. Bin Laden and al-Turabi, and possibly Iran, were believed to be behind these attacks, which experts say were staged to show that Americans stationed in Muslim countries would not be safe, even in their protected facilities.

After the Saudi Arabia attacks, the United States pressured the rulers in Sudan to crack down on al-Turabi. The Sudanese government arrested and jailed al-Turabi, and Bin Laden moved his operations again, this time to Afghanistan. That country, following the Soviet withdrawal, had fallen into the hands of an Islamist group called the Taliban, which imposed strict Islamic rule. Bin Laden and al-Turabi were financial supporters of the Taliban, and the Afghans agreed to provide Bin Laden a refuge. In this secure place, with al-Turabi no longer an active partner, Bin Laden organized an international jihadist network that he called al Qaeda, the Arabic word for base. Here, Bin Laden trained and financed scores of terrorist fighters and coordinated a series of attacks on the United States.

AL QAEDA PROBLEM IS BIGGER THAN OSAMA BIN LADEN

"[Osama bin Laden is] not the only source of the problem, obviously. . . . If you killed him tomorrow, you'd still have a problem with al-Qaeda." —Dick Cheney, vice president of the United States.

Quoted in *Fort Worth Star-Telegram*, "General Plays Down Value of Capturing Bin Laden," February 24, 2007, p. A08.

In August 1998, for example, al Qaeda used truck bombs to attack U.S. embassies in Nairobi, Kenya, and Dar es Salaam, Tanzania, killing 224 people. In October 2000, al Qaeda agents bombed the USS *Cole*, a U.S. ship docked in Yemen, killing 17 soldiers. Two other possible attacks were thwarted by authori-

This makeshift memorial remembers those who were killed in the al Qaeda-sponsored terrorist bombing in London, England, on July 7, 2005.

ties during these years, including a December 1999 plot to bomb millennium celebrations in Seattle, Washington. Of course, the attack that won Bin Laden the most media attention was the September 11, 2001, double strike on the World Trade Center and the Pentagon that killed 2,974 people, wounded many others, and left Americans in a state of shock and anger.

The 9/11 attacks marked the beginning of the U.S. war on terror, but al Qaeda and affiliated terrorist groups have continued to attack numerous American and western targets overseas. In 2002, for example, five attacks were attributed to al Qaeda, including bombings of a nightclub frequented by tourists in Bali, Indonesia, that killed 202 people. In 2003, the terrorism continued and included bombings of a housing compound in Riyadh, Saudi Arabia (51 dead), suicide car bombs at a Marriott Hotel in Jakarta, Indonesia (12 dead), and the bombing of two synagogues in Istanbul, Turkey (25 dead). The next year, 2004, began with a March attack during the morning rush hour in Madrid, Spain, that killed 202 and injured more than 1,400, and continued with a series of attacks on various sites in Saudi Arabia that killed 28 people, including Paul Johnson Jr., an American who was first taken hostage. In 2005 bombs were exploded on three trains and a bus in London, England, killing 52 people, and tourist sites in Bali, Indonesia, and Amman, Jordan, were attacked, killing a total of 79 people.

Al Qaeda in Iraq

In recent years, according to most experts, Iraq has become the new center for al Qaeda terrorism. In fact, after the U.S. invasion of Iraq in 2003, Islamic militants flocked to Iraq to fight U.S. forces just as they came to fight the Soviets in Afghanistan a decade earlier. Today, al Qaeda in Iraq (AQI) is led by Abu Ayyub al-Masri, an Egyptian; his predecessor, Jordanian Abu Musab al Zarqawi, was killed by U.S. soldiers. The group's goal is to sow sectarian violence—that is, fighting between Iraq's Shia and Sunni Muslims—in order to disrupt U.S. efforts to set up an Iraqi democracy, create instability in the country, and force American troops to go home. As Lionel Beehner of the Council on Foreign Relations explains:

> [AQI] aims to topple the . . . government in Iraq by attacking Shiites [or Shias], particularly those who have collaborated with the United States, whether they are civilians, army soldiers, or police officers, primarily in and around Baghdad. . . . Some of the more radical members of al-Qaeda favor the installment of a caliphate —or Islamic government—in Iraq. Short of that, they seek a safe haven from which al-Qaeda can recruit and train terrorists.[24]

AQI is said to be responsible for countless suicide bomb and improvised explosive device (IED) attacks in Iraq, including a shocking 2006 bombing of the ancient, gold-domed Al Askari mosque in Samarra, Iraq—the third holiest Shia shrine—that sparked a marked increase in the number of Shia-Sunni sectarian attacks. Iraq has now become al Qaeda's training ground, where jihadists learn to become experienced fighters and then return to wage jihad in their homelands. Indeed, U.S. general David Petraeus, the head of the U.S. military effort, has stated

Osama bin Laden, the leader of al Qaeda, has managed to hide from authorities for years, while still operating his terrorist organization from remote locations in the Middle East.

that "Iraq is . . . the central front of al Qaeda's global [terrorist] campaign."[25]

A Broad Movement

Meanwhile, although U.S. forces defeated the pro–al Qaeda Taliban government in Afghanistan and removed al Qaeda operations there, Bin Laden was able to escape and establish a new base of operations in a rugged, mountainous region in Pakistan, near the Afghanistan border. There, he is protected from Pakistani troops by local tribal leaders, and the United States is reluctant to invade the area for fear of angering the Pakistani government and the rest of the Muslim world. From this position, Bin Laden now runs a prolific propaganda campaign that has made him the symbol for the global jihadist movement. According to Middle East expert Bruce Reidel, al Qaeda puts out numerous videos and "some 4,500 overtly jihadi Web sites . . . [to] disseminate the al Qaeda leadership's messages."[26]

Al Qaeda has now expanded its operations throughout the Muslim world and even into Europe. In fact, according to some experts, the United Kingdom has become a focal point for al Qaeda recruitment because of the large numbers of Pakistani immigrants living in Britain and the easy access between the two countries. One of the most notable signs of this al Qaeda presence was the July 7, 2005, attack on the London public transport system.

This expansion of al Qaeda means the United States remains vulnerable to terrorist attacks. As former U.S. director of national intelligence John Negroponte reported in January 2007, al Qaeda's core elements "continue to plot attacks against our homeland and other targets, with the objective of inflicting mass casualties. And they are cultivating stronger operational connections and relationships that radiate outward from their leaders' secure hideout in Pakistan to affiliates throughout the Middle East, North Africa, and Europe."[27]

MOTIVATIONS, TACTICS, AND TARGETS

The media and politicians often portray terrorists as evildoers or crazy lunatics, but interviews with individual terrorists and studies of terrorist groups suggest that terrorism is not irrational. Instead, experts have concluded that most terrorists are motivated by feelings of revenge or a desire to right an injustice, and most terrorist attacks are carefully planned and executed to achieve specific political, religious, or ideological goals. In certain cases, terrorists have been successful in achieving their stated aims, and some have even been elected into government leadership positions.

Ordinary Terrorists

The news media loves to cover dramatic events, so terrorist strikes are extensively reported on television and other media outlets. However, this coverage often focuses on the sensational and horrific aspects of the event and portrays terrorists as crazed killers, giving viewers little information or background on the terrorists' objectives. Politicians, too, often respond by calling terrorism evil or suggesting that terrorists have no rational reasons for their violence. Shortly after the 9/11 terrorist attacks, for example, U.S. president George W. Bush stated:

> [Terrorists] hate our freedoms—our freedom of religion, our freedom of speech, our freedom to vote and assemble and disagree with each other. . . . These terrorists kill not merely to end lives, but to disrupt and end a way of life. . . . With every atrocity, they hope that America grows fearful, retreating from the world and forsaking

Most terrorism experts reject the idea that all terrorists are crazy, evil, or irrational. It has been found that many terrorists come from ordinary backgrounds. Shown here are 8 of 17 suspected terrorists from the 2004 Madrid, Spain, bombing.

our friends. They stand against us, because we stand in their way. We are not deceived by their pretenses to piety. We have seen their kind before. They are the heirs of all the murderous ideologies of the 20th century. By sacrificing human life to serve their radical visions—by abandoning every value except the will to power—they follow in the path of fascism, and Nazism, and totalitarianism.[28]

However, most terrorism experts reject the idea that terrorists are crazy, evil, or irrational. Dr. Andrew Silke, a United Nations adviser and forensic psychologist at Britain's Leicester University, explains: "The widespread view that terrorists are isolated, vulnerable young men with paranoid or borderline personality disorders is false. . . . Psychologists who have met a terrorist face to face . . . actually find them to be fairly ordinary."[29] Indeed, all of the al Qaeda members studied by Silke came from middle- or upper-class backgrounds, two-thirds were college-educated, many had postgraduate degrees, and seven out of ten were married with children.

Reporter Terry McDermott reached the same conclusion. In his book about the 9/11 bombers called *Perfect Soldiers*, he notes that most of the nineteen al Qaeda hijackers responsible for the September 11 attacks on the United States came from "unexceptional backgrounds"[30] that would never suggest the violence that accompanied their deaths. Mohammed Atta, the pilot of the first plane to hit the World Trade Center, for example, grew up in a middle-class family in Egypt and had done graduate work in architecture. Marwan al-Shehhi, the pilot of the second plane in New York, was a member of the United Arab Emirates army. Hani Hanjour, the pilot of the plane that crashed into the Pentagon, was a friendly and polite Saudi who spent a lot of time surfing the Internet. Ziad al-Jarrah, the pilot of a fourth plane

RELIGIOUS FANATICISM INSPIRING TERRORISM IS NOT NEW

"The connection between religion and terrorism is not new. More than two thousand years ago the first acts of what we now describe as 'terrorism' were perpetrated by religious fanatics." —Bruce Hoffman, professor of security studies at Georgetown University's Edmund A. Walsh School of Foreign Service and a recognized expert on terrorism.

Bruce Hoffman, *Inside Terrorism*. New York: Columbia University Press, 1998, p. 88.

that crashed in Pennsylvania, was happily married and grew up in a nonreligious, middle-class, westernized Lebanese family. McDermott explains that these men slowly "evolved into devout, pious young men who, over time, drew deeper and deeper into Islam, . . . [and eventually] saw themselves as soldiers of God."[31]

People tend to demonize terrorists because they do not want to justify actions that are so horrible and incomprehensible. As terrorism expert Stephen Sloan explains, there is a "public perception . . . that what the terrorists do is not rational. . . . [and] ascribing rationality to an action is viewed as justifying it."[32] The same psychological process often takes place during war, when the enemy is dehumanized in every possible way. In truth, however, most experts believe that terrorism is not mindless, but rather highly planned and organized violence that is used as a tool to accomplish a larger objective. As Sloan says, "Terrorism is purposeful violence . . . a means to an end and a way to achieve various goals."[33]

Revenge and Retribution

The specific goals and motivations for terrorism, however, vary from one individual terrorist to another and among different terrorist groups. At the individual level, experts say, many terrorists are driven by a thirst for revenge for some real or perceived injustice. Terrorism lecturer and author Louise Richardson says conversations with individual terrorists have shown that they often have a very simple, black-and-white view of the world and commit violent acts as retribution for some suffering they have witnessed within their ethnic, religious, or political group. Richardson explains: "Terrorists see themselves as working heroically for the benefit of others, not for themselves. In this way they see themselves as morally distinguishable from criminals out for their own gain. . . . They see themselves as defending the weak against the strong and punishing the strong for their violation of all moral codes."[34]

Terrorism expert Bruce Hoffman agrees; he explains that, unlike a common criminal who is motivated by greed or some personal grievance, "the terrorist is fundamentally an altruist: he believes that he is serving a 'good' cause designed to achieve a greater good for a wider constituency . . . [that] the terrorist or his organization purport to represent."[35]

Sometimes terrorists are radicalized by witnessing, either in person or through television or film, a specific act of injustice. Richardson gives numerous examples of terrorists who have ex-

Peace in Northern Ireland

On May 8, 2007, two enemies joined together to form a power-sharing government in Northern Ireland—an event that many people think marked the end of terrorism and the beginning of an era of peace for the region. As CNN's European political editor Robin Oakley said in a May 9, 2007, online article, "We can say this is that day that politics takes over from terrorism here in Northern Ireland." Northern Ireland had been the site of a decades-long struggle between the Catholics and Protestants. On the Catholic side was the Irish Republican Army (IRA) and its political counterpart Sinn Fein, groups often labeled as terrorist, which fought to unite Northern and Southern Ireland and gain independence from British rule. On the other side were mostly Protestant Democratic Union Party (DUP) loyalists who wanted Northern Ireland to remain under British control. At the May 8 ceremony these groups were represented, respectively, by Sinn Fein leader Martin McGuinness and Democratic Unionist Party leader Ian Paisley. Paisley was sworn in as the Northern Ireland assembly's first minister, and McGuinness became deputy first minister. Under the new government, Northern Ireland will have self-rule but will remain part of the United Kingdom.

CNN, "Northern Ireland Begins 'New Era,'" May 9, 2007. www.cnn.com/2007/WORLD/europe/05/08/north ern.ireland/index.html.

plained how they were awakened by the sight or story of atrocities inflicted on innocent people. For example, Vellupillai Prabakharan, the leader of the Sri Lankan Tamil Tigers terrorist group, has said: "It is the plight of the Tamil people that compelled me to take up arms . . . the ruthless manner in which our people were murdered, massacred, maimed."[36] And Richardson explains that "once a person becomes involved in violence the grievances to be avenged multiply and the opportunities for and means of vengeance expand dramatically."[37] A prime example is the Arab-Israeli conflict, in which the violence on both sides creates a vicious cycle that fuels an endless stream of Palestinians seeking revenge followed by repeated Israeli retaliations.

In other cases, experts suggest, terrorism may be rooted in decades of oppression and poverty, and the deep frustration and hatred generated by those conditions. Some commentators, for example, believe that the failure of Middle Eastern Arab nations to provide for their poor, combined with highly autocratic and corrupt leadership in many of these countries, has helped to fuel al Qaeda and other jihadist terrorism. Osama bin Laden, just weeks after the September 11 terrorist attacks, suggested that this may be part of his motivation:

> Here is America struck by God Almighty in one of its vital organs, so that its greatest buildings are destroyed. Grace and gratitude to God. America has been filled with horror from north to south and east to west, and thanks be to God that what America is tasting now is only a copy of what we have tasted. Our Islamic nation has been tasting the same for more than 80 years, humiliation and disgrace, its sons killed and their blood spilled, its sanctities desecrated.[38]

Bin Laden and many other terrorists thus see themselves as victims, not aggressors, and their outrage over what they perceive as deep injustices enables them to commit acts that go far beyond what might be considered justifiable violence by most people. As Harvard University lecturer and U.S. terrorism expert Jessica Stern has explained, "Because [terrorists] believe their cause is just, and because the population they hope to protect is purportedly so deprived, abused, and helpless, they persuade themselves that any action—even a heinous crime—is justified. They know they are right, not just politically, but morally."[39]

The Role of Terrorist Groups

Most terrorism experts agree, however, that the majority of terrorism violence is inflicted by terrorist organizations rather than lone individuals acting on their own initiative. Often led by charismatic leaders such as Osama bin Laden, these groups recruit receptive individuals and then stoke their feelings of anger and revenge in order to create an organized force to carry out the group's terrorist agenda.

Sometimes, the leaders of terrorist groups have higher educations and come from wealthier backgrounds than those recruited as followers. Stern has criticized certain Middle East terrorist groups for actively preying upon the poor and the ignorant to carry out suicide bombing missions. Some Palestinian groups, Stern claims, fund schools or orphanages for the poor and then recruit young men from these institutions into their terrorist operations. She explains, "These foot soldiers often function as cannon fodder, with minimal training."[40] Many of the Islamist jihadist groups, on the other hand, appear to attract more educated and well-off followers, and provide them with more intensive and advanced training. Psychiatrist and terrorism researcher Marc Sageman, for example, looked at 172 members of al Qaeda and found that two-thirds were middle or

In some areas of the world it is not unusual to see pro-terrorist propaganda, such as this poster of a Palestinian suicide bomber, on public display.

upper class, 60 percent had attended college, and many had advanced degrees. Al Qaeda's global operations appear to require educated volunteers who can successfully integrate into affluent, western societies without being noticed.

Richardson explains that the most enduring and successful terrorist groups tend to be those with close ties to their communities, and whose values and goals are supported by their own societies. In these situations, community members often encourage what they view as an armed struggle for their rights, and in such a society joining a terrorist group can appear to be one of the noblest actions a young man or woman can take. This pattern is clearly seen among the Palestinians, where children as young as six or seven express the desire to grow up to be martyrs—suicide bombers for the Palestinian cause.

Political Motivations

Given the tendency of many terrorist groups to identify with societal grievances, a number of experts have concluded that the majority of terrorists are politically motivated. Hoffman, for example, believes that all terrorism is essentially political, or "the deliberate creation and exploitation of fear through violence or the threat of violence in the pursuit of political change."[41] He explains that violence or the threat of violence is always used as a means to achieve power because terrorists "are unswervingly convinced that only through violence can their cause triumph and their long-term political aims be attained."[42] Ultimately, Hoffman believes, most terrorists seek the power and authority to take specific actions, whether it be the overthrow of a government, a redistribution of wealth, changes in state boundaries, vindication of minority rights, or the establishment of religious rule.

University of Chicago political scientist Robert Pape agrees that political motivations are behind much of today's terrorism. Pape, who compiled an extensive database on suicide terrorism for a 2005 book on the subject, concluded that almost all modern suicide terrorist attacks share one common goal, "to compel modern democracies to withdraw military forces from territory that the terrorists consider to be their homeland."[43] According

Most modern terrorist groups band together around the idea of nationalism, or the independence of their people and lands from what they view as oppressive governments. For example, Chechen rebels, pictured, fight for the independence of Chechnya from Russia.

to Pape, "the taproot of suicide terrorism is nationalism,"[44] and suicide terror is "an extreme strategy for national liberation"[45] that allows terrorists to be viewed by their supporters as martyrs for a higher cause.

Pape sees this pattern in most contemporary terrorist movements. He says Hezbollah, for example, fought to force Israel out of Lebanon in the 1980s, and that Palestinian terrorist groups now push for Israel to withdraw from the occupied territories (homelands claimed by Palestinians). Similarly, Pape argues that terrorist groups in Sri Lanka and Chechnya also both fight for nationalist causes, demanding independence for their people and lands from what they view as oppressive governments. Pape believes that al Qaeda terrorism fits this model as well. He points out that Bin Laden is obsessed with the presence of American combat forces in the Muslim world, first in Saudi Arabia following the Iraqi invasion of Kuwait, and now in Iraq. As Pape sees it, "Al-Qaeda is . . . a cross-national military alliance of national liberation movements working together against what they see as a common imperial threat."[46]

Religious Terrorism

The recent rise of Islamic fundamentalist terrorism, however, has caused many other scholars to suggest that religion is an equally important part of today's terrorist attacks. Often, these religious terrorists seem to have both religious and political goals, or putting it another way, political goals that may be driven by religious motives. Sageman, for example, believes that a

Indonesian Muslims gather in Jakarta in 2000 to offer their services in a jihad (holy war) against Christians in Indonesia.

growing number of Muslims, disturbed by the creep of western influences into the Islamic world, seek essentially religious goals—the expulsion of western and secular influences, the reestablishment of a fundamentalist version of Islam, and the creation of Islamic governments that will strictly enforce core, conservative Islamic values. Some Muslims want to use peaceful means to achieve these goals, but the creation and spread of al Qaeda in recent years has galvanized a new, much more militant movement. As Sageman explains, "The global [Islamic] jihad is a worldwide revivalist movement with the goal of reestablishing past Muslim glory in a great Islamist state stretching from Morocco to the Philippines."[47]

TERRORISM IS A TACTIC OF THE WEAK

"Terrorism is not an enemy; it is a method of using violence to gain political objectives. Its tactics are usually employed by weaker, irregular groups against governments that possess organized armies and the modern means for waging war formally and more destructively." —William Greider, a political journalist and national affairs correspondent for *The Nation*, a progressive magazine.

William Greider, "Under the Banner of the 'War' on Terror," *The Nation*, June 21, 2004. www.thenation.com/doc/20040621/greider/.

Ideally, these jihadists would like to have a large army that could be used to launch a massive military strike against their enemies, but they lack this type of military capacity. Instead, they use terrorism as a means to instill fear among secular Muslims and westerners and motivate them to change government policies. As terrorism experts Monte Palmer and Princess Palmer state, "The jihadist war plan is overwhelmingly psychological. Terror is the jihadist instrument of choice for creating fear and chaos among their adversaries, be they Americans or errant Muslims."[48]

Despite its lack of military might, this jihadist terror campaign has been one of the most lethal in the history of terrorism. As Hoffman explains, "Terrorism motivated in whole or in part by religious imperatives has often led to more intense acts of violence that have produced considerably higher levels of fatalities than . . . [those] perpetrated by secular terrorist organizations."[49] In fact, in the last two decades, experts say the most serious and deadly terrorism attacks have all been committed in the name of religion, many of them by al Qaeda's global jihadist movement.

Experts say religious terrorists tend to be more violent than secular terrorists because religion justifies large-scale killing by calling it a sacred act. As Hoffman puts it, "For the religious terrorist, violence is . . . a divine duty executed in direct response to some theological demand or imperative. . . . [Terrorists] are consequently unconstrained by the political, moral or practical constraints that may . . . [stop secular terrorists from] indiscriminate killing on a massive scale."[50] Hoffman explains that religious terrorists often are alienated from mainstream society and see themselves as involved in total war that seeks to eliminate anyone who is not a member of the terrorists' religion or religious sect. Because they seek deep fundamental changes in social or political systems, they see no reason for behaving reasonably in order to gain the support of ordinary people or to preserve parts of the existing order. Of course, most religious terrorists also believe strongly in an afterlife, so they often lose their own fear of death. Many experts worry that they may even consider undertaking massively destructive actions that could potentially destroy the earth or many of its inhabitants.

The Logic of Terrorism

Whatever their motivations, most experts agree that terrorists use terror tactics for purely practical and logical reasons—because they do not have access to conventional military resources or manpower. Moreover, terrorist attacks are a highly effective method of fighting countries or governments that do have massive armies and equipment. Instead of engaging a large army on the battlefield, where they would lose, terrorist groups use asymmetric warfare tactics such as assassinations, kidnappings, hostage-takings, and suicide bombings as a way to level the playing field.

Several methods of terrorism—assassinations, kidnappings, hostage-takings, and suicide bombings—are inexpensive yet effective ways for terrorist groups to gain attention for their cause.

Terrorist attacks are also relatively cheap and easily affordable for small terrorist organizations with limited budgets. In fact, many commentators have called suicide terrorism the ultimate strategic weapon of the poor and the weak since it inflicts high casualties at such a low cost. Compared to conventional armies, which require billions of dollars' worth of high-tech equipment and personnel, a suicide bombing requires only a willing martyr, a little training and planning, and a few inexpensive bomb parts. Even the dramatic and complicated 9/11 attack, according to experts, cost only about $500,000.

Terrorist attacks work by generating widespread media publicity—the more spectacular the attack, the greater the media attention it garners. Groups such as al Qaeda clearly utilize this tactic that early terrorists called "propaganda of the deed." Bin Laden considers the 9/11 attack his crowning achievement because of its high shock value, the numbers of people killed, and the symbolism of the targets—the World Trade Center, the center of western finances and economics, and the Pentagon, the heart of the U.S. military establishment. Modern terrorist groups such as al Qaeda also like to target civilians, not only because they are easy targets, but also because the deaths of civilians typically generate the most public outrage and publicity.

RELIGION MOTIVATES SUICIDE ATTACKS

"Suicide attacks . . . are now mostly religiously motivated actions by small, loosely connected groups to exorcise [eliminate] cultural humiliation, of which military occupation may be just one manifestation [form]." —Scott Atran, research director at the National Center for Scientific Research in Paris.

Quoted in Stefan Lovgren, "Suicide Attacks Evolving, Increasing," *National Geographic News*, July 29, 2005. http://news.nationalgeographic.com/news/2005/07/0729_050729 _suicide.html.

Terrorists hope, by instilling society-wide fear and terror, they can eventually weaken the will of the government and force political or other concessions. Sometimes, the concession sought is specific, such as the release of imprisoned comrades. In other cases, the goal is broader and much less direct. The IRA in Northern Ireland, for example, sought to make the region chaotic and ungovernable, as a way of forcing British police and troops to leave and grant them the right of self-governance. Similarly, Palestinian attacks on Israel are designed to make the Israeli occupation of Palestinian territories too costly, in order to force an Israeli retreat and pave the way for the creation of a Palestinian state. Experts believe al Qaeda's current campaign against the United States, too, is aimed at forcing changes in U.S. foreign policy such as withdrawal of troops and a reduced presence in the Middle East.

The Effectiveness of Terrorism

Some commentators suggest that part of the appeal of terrorism is that it has been successful for some groups, helping them reach political or strategic goals. Some terrorist groups have even acquired political legitimacy and governing power. The classic example is that of the IRA, whose terrorist bomb tactics eventually bore fruit by attaining self-rule for Northern Ireland. The Sri Lankan Tamil Tigers, too, won a measure of success after a terrorist campaign against government troops and supporters. Although violence has recently re-emerged, in February 2002 the group signed an agreement with the government of Sri Lanka that called for a cease-fire of hostilities and peace talks.

Similarly, most analysts credit Hezbollah suicide attacks with forcing the withdrawal of foreign troops from Lebanon in the early 1980s. These successes, in turn, paved the way for Hezbollah to participate in elections and become a mainstream political party in Lebanon. Terrorist strikes also seem to have helped to achieve some of the aims of Palestinian extremist

Pictured is the aftermath of a 1996 Hamas-sponsored suicide bombing in Israel. Ten years later, Hamas candidates won the majority of seats in the Palestinian parliament.

groups such as Hamas, which has been successful at derailing PLO-negotiated peace settlements it viewed as unacceptable. Like Hezbollah, Hamas has converted its terrorist campaign into electoral power, winning a majority of seats in the Palestinian parliament in 2006.

Many other terrorist groups, however, have not come close to accomplishing their stated goals. Despite terrorist campaigns by various groups, for example, the Palestinians remain in a conflict with Israel over its continuing occupation and the creation of a Palestinian state. Similarly, the Basques in Spain have never won independence despite many decades of attacks; the PKK in Turkey has yet to establish a Kurdistan nation; and the Chechens have been repeatedly overpowered by Russian government forces and denied their nationalist dreams. Some commentators, in fact, suggest that nonviolence has been equally or more effective than terrorism in advancing political and humanitarian causes. As Australian professor Brian Martin explains:

Hezbollah's Political Strength

Hezbollah, a Shia Islamist group in Lebanon that reportedly receives support from the Iranian government, is listed as a terrorist group by the United States. The group was one of the first to use suicide bombings against Israel, and the U.S. government holds the group responsible for bombing military barracks housing U.S. and French troops stationed in Lebanon in 1983 during the Lebanon-Israeli war. Hezbollah seeks to establish an Islamic government in Lebanon and to eliminate Israel, which it sees as an illegitimate state. Many Lebanese and others in the Arab world, however, see Hezbollah as a defender of Lebanon and a legitimate force of resistance against Israeli aggression. The group holds 14 of the 128 seats in the Lebanese parliament and sponsors a variety of hospitals, schools, and social programs in the country. In 2006, after Hezbollah fired rockets and missiles into Israel, Israel responded with air attacks and a ground invasion of southern Lebanon. The conflict lasted 34 days, killed hundreds of mostly Lebanese civilians, and caused significant infrastructure damage. However, it failed to settle the differences between the two sides. Today, Hezbollah remains a strong force in southern Lebanon, both politically and militarily.

There are many examples where nonviolent action has been effective in situations where violence did not or could not have succeeded. The East Timorese armed struggle against the Indonesian military occupation made little headway over many years, . . . [but] after the liberation movement switched its emphasis from armed struggle in the countryside to nonviolent protest in the cities, it was able to stimulate much greater international support, eventually leading to independence. . . . [And] in South Africa, armed struggle did little to undermine apartheid. It was only when the challenge to apartheid shifted largely to nonviolent means that great progress was made.[51]

As a way to create enduring political change, therefore, terrorism appears to have a mixed record.

CHAPTER 4

TERRORISM'S HIGH COSTS

While producing sometimes limited gains in terms of political or societal changes sought by terrorist groups, terrorism can be expensive for the overall society. These costs include not only loss and injury to innocent lives, but also economic costs such as reduced tourism and other business disruptions, and skyrocketing costs for counterterrorism, security, and military measures. Many experts say the dearest price of terrorism, however, is the increased police power and corresponding cutbacks on civil liberties enacted by governments to deal with terrorist threats—actions that many experts fear might erode freedoms and privileges important to democratic societies.

The Human Effects

The most immediate cost of terrorism is a human one—measured in civilian lives lost and injured by terrorist attacks. Historically, terrorism has not produced large numbers of deaths or injuries; until recently, many terrorist groups sought to limit casualties for fear of alienating the public. According to a U.S. government report, *Patterns of Global Terrorism*, for example, only 405 persons were killed and only 791 were wounded by terrorist attacks around the world in the year 2000. This pattern changed somewhat with the advent of Islamic jihadist terrorism. Although the total numbers of people killed or hurt by terrorism worldwide has not increased greatly as compared to previous years, on a number of recent occasions jihadists have succeeded in inflicting massive civilian casualties and damage during spectacular, large-scale attacks.

In the case of the 9/11 attacks, for example, there were 2,974 confirmed fatalities, not including the 19 hijackers. Most of the people who died were in the World Trade Center and in the Pentagon and killed instantly when the buildings were hit by terrorist-piloted planes; others died later of smoke inhalation or jumped to their deaths to avoid fire. Still others were emergency workers who rushed into the chaos. Twenty-four people were listed as missing, because no trace of them was ever found. Except for the Pentagon employees, all of the people killed were civilians.

A majority of those who survived the New York attack, a total of about seventy-one thousand people who either worked

The 9/11 terrorist attacks against the United States were crafted to cause as many civilian deaths as possible. Nearly 3,000 people lost their lives in the attacks, and countless others were injured.

in the vicinity of the World Trade Center or who happened to be in the area at the time, suffered injuries, some of them life-changing and ultimately life-threatening. Interviews with more than eight thousand of these survivors by the U.S. Centers for Disease Control and Prevention (CDC) suggest that over 43 percent suffered some type of physical injury on the day of the attack, most typically eye injuries, and more than half of all survivors were still suffering from some type of respiratory problem two years later.

In addition to physical injuries, such as lung damage, many 9/11 responders suffer from emotional injuries as a result of witnessing the destruction at Ground Zero. Here, paramedic and 9/11 responder Marvin Bethea shows the medication he has to take since the September 11 terrorist attack.

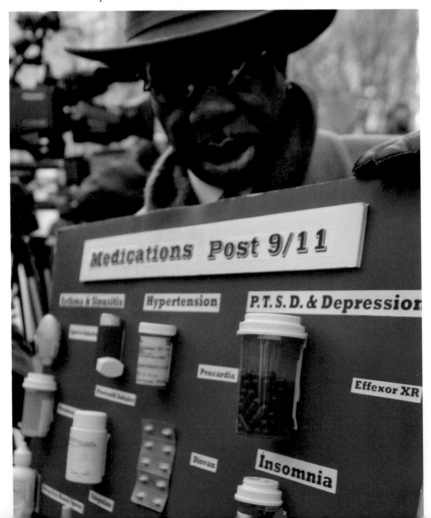

Indeed, the highly toxic fumes created by the blast in New York City have left a legacy of death and illness. Many local residents continue today to suffer from persistent respiratory ailments as a result of breathing in asbestos and other deadly toxins during the aftermath of the terrorist attack. In addition, approximately forty thousand people—including firefighters, police officers, and other workers—were involved in rescue and cleanup during or after 9/11, and thousands of these are now reporting serious illnesses such as cancer and pulmonary fibrosis. Some are dying or have already died from their illnesses.

Another legacy of the 9/11 attack is a rash of mental injuries, including anxiety, depression, and post-traumatic stress syn-

MORE FUNDING NEEDED FOR HOMELAND SECURITY

"Homeland security is seriously underfunded. Whole areas of the homeland security budget—such as port security, first responders, and border security—need much larger infusions of money and personnel." —Joshua S. Goldstein, an associate of the Watson Institute for International Studies at Brown University and a leading expert on war.

Joshua S. Goldstein, *The Real Price of War: How You Pay for the War on Terror*. New York: New York University Press, 2004, p. 185.

drome (PTS; also sometimes called post-traumatic stress disorder, or PTSD)—a condition in which the patient keeps reliving a highly stressful event. Common symptoms of PTS include profound sadness or fear; distressing thoughts, feelings, or images of the event; inability to sleep; frightening dreams; and problems with concentration. First responders or bystanders who witnessed the collapse of buildings or the death or injury of others are the most likely candidates for PTS, but studies have shown that many other people not directly affected by the incident may also experience trauma. Children, people with preexisting mental illness, or persons living near the area of the strike, for example, may fear that they or their families will become victims of a future attack. In fact, the American Psychological Association (APA) Task Force on Resilience in Response to Terror says that even people who simply watched television coverage of the 9/11 attacks reported feeling a high level of stress. Altogether, according to one estimate, 422,000 New Yorkers were afflicted with PTS trauma symptoms as a result of the tragedy, and countless other Americans began to live with a heightened sense of fear and anxiety.

Property and Economic Damages

In addition to the trail of deaths and injuries, terrorist events produce significant economic damages. Following 9/11, for example, the U.S. Congress created the September 11th Victim Compensation Fund of 2001 to compensate the families of people killed or injured on the day of the attacks. Within three years of the attacks, the fund had distributed $7 billion to the 9/11 victims. Due to the respiratory and mental trauma issues that have come to light in recent years, however, injury costs are expected to increase. New York mayor Michael Bloomberg has estimated, for example, that the cost of caring for city workers who become ill as a result of 9/11 will be approximately $393 million a year. Bloomberg wants the 9/11 fund to be reopened to compensate those who suffer from long-term health effects.

Terrorist attacks also typically cause property damage. Experts say the September 11 attacks inflicted more material damage than any previous terrorist attack. Both of the twin towers of the World Trade Center, each with 110 floors, were completely destroyed, and many other surrounding buildings were either destroyed or seriously damaged. The cost of replacing and restoring these buildings, and repairing the damage done to public works, infrastructure (such as streets, utilities, subways), police cars, fire trucks, and ambulances, was astronomical. According to an August 2002 estimate prepared by economist Robert Looney, "The destruction of physical assets was estimated . . . to amount to $14 billion for private businesses, $1.5 billion for state and local government enterprises and $0.7 billion for federal enterprises. Rescue, cleanup, and related costs have been estimated to amount to at least $11 bil-

The September 11 attacks inflicted more material damage than any previous terrorist attack. Damage and clean-up costs at the Pentagon alone swelled to about $576 million.

lion for a total direct cost of $27.2 billion."[52] Insurance companies were hit especially hard; they paid out a total of $34 billion in insured losses, a figure that covered part of the damage to buildings and infrastructure.

On top of these costs, a number of city businesses were forced to close their doors, and as many as 200,000 people lost their jobs. The tourism industry was particularly affected; during the week after the attack, hotel occupancy in the city fell below 40 percent and 3,000 employees were laid off. One estimate found that the total economic loss to the city in the month following the attack was $105 billion.

The U.S. and world economy also suffered losses. The New York Stock Exchange, the nation's largest securities trading entity, was closed for six days, and when it reopened the Dow Jones industrial average (the most widely used stock market indicator)

The Terrorism Risk Assurance Act (TRIA)

The damage caused by the 9/11 terrorist attacks caused many insurance companies to drop coverage for terrorism, creating a situation in which many businesses could no longer purchase insurance against terrorist attacks. To remedy this problem and help the insurance industry recover from 9/11 losses, President George W. Bush on November 26, 2002, signed into law the Terrorism Risk Insurance Act (TRIA). This law required property and casualty insurers doing business in the United States to offer coverage for acts of terrorism, and in return, the federal government agreed to reinsure, or pay for, a large percentage of any such losses. The act defined an "act of terrorism" as any act dangerous to human life, property, or infrastructure that results in more than $5 million damage ($100 million in 2007) within the United States or on U.S. property, committed by a foreigner or someone acting for a foreign interest. Under the law, insurers paid a portion of their losses before federal assistance was available; the federal government then paid about 90 percent of remaining terrorism losses and the insurer paid the rest. The act was due to expire in December 2007 but was extended for another seven years.

had dropped 684.81 points. The nation also lost four civilian aircraft valued at $385 million and incurred damage and cleanup costs of about $576 million at the Pentagon. Moreover, the entire U.S. air transportation network was shut down for two and a half days—at a loss of $1.5 billion in lost airfares and cargo shipping fees. In fact, for about a year the entire worldwide economy slowed. As trade specialist Dick K. Nanto noted in a 2004 report, "Most of the world dropped into a synchronous recession —from 4.1% world economic growth in 2000 to 1.4% in 2001."[53] Altogether, according to conservative estimates, the September 11, 2001, terrorist attacks cost the United States and the world hundreds of billions of dollars in economic losses.

Homeland Security Costs

The short-term economic losses, however, pale in comparison to the long-term costs of responding to the new terror threat exposed by the 9/11 attacks. Following September 11, the U.S. government responded with a series of expensive counterterrorism measures. As a first step, the government spent billions on high-technology equipment to screen for weapons and bombs at airports, harbors, and federal sites. Most of these funds were spent on new baggage screening equipment required by the 2001 Aviation and Transportation Security Act. Additional monies were spent on other aspects of transportation security—to hire a new workforce of airport screeners; retrofit aircraft with antiterrorist devices; train armed air marshals to ride along on random flights; and secure federal buildings, seaports, and borders. The total cost of these programs has been estimated at $41 billion.

The government also created a huge new federal department, called Homeland Security, to oversee the various domestic antiterrorist programs designed to deter and respond to future suicide terror strikes. As reporter Angie C. Marek explains, "It was

To beef up security at U.S. airports following the 9/11 attacks, the Department of Homeland Security authorized billions of dollars for high-technology equipment to screen for weapons and bombs.

the single largest reorganization of the federal government since the creation of the Department of Defense, in 1947."[54] Since 2001, huge expenditures have been made in the name of homeland security, and the budget seems to grow substantially each year. In fiscal year 2000, for example, the United States spent only $13 billion on homeland security, but the Department of Homeland Security's budget for 2007 was $42.8 billion, an increase of more than 300 percent. For 2008 the department requested $46.4 billion, an 8 percent increase over the previous year.

Businesses—from owners of office buildings to companies that could be targeted by terrorism—also found themselves spending more money for terrorism-related security after 9/11. These costs included better locks; more security guards, surveillance cameras, equipment, and software; and more employee time spent purchasing and maintaining these systems. Another routine business cost, terrorism insurance for property,

PER HOUSEHOLD COST OF THE WAR

"About $500 per month is what the government spends, per household, on war-related budgets, including veterans' benefits and homeland security expenses." —Joshua S. Goldstein, an associate of the Watson Institute for International Studies at Brown University and a leading expert on war.

Joshua S. Goldstein, *The Real Price of War: How You Pay for the War on Terror*, New York: New York University Press, 2004, p. 22.

either became unavailable or the costs soared following the events of 2001. In 2002 the government guaranteed terrorism coverage, so in the event of another terrorist attack taxpayers may foot much of the bill.

The Cost of the U.S. War on Terror

Terrorism, and the anger and panic it produces among the public, also often prompts governments to undertake expensive military actions to show that they are protecting national security and exacting revenge for terrorist attacks. Just days after the September 11 attacks, for example, U.S. president George W.

Bush declared a war on terrorism, promising to track down Osama bin Laden and use every resource and tool to disrupt and defeat the terrorism threat. This effort began less than a month later, on October 7, 2001, when the United States attacked Afghanistan's Taliban government, which was accused of harboring al Qaeda terrorists. In an action that received widespread support from the American public, U.S. troops destroyed al Qaeda bases in Afghanistan, ousted the pro–al Qaeda Taliban government, and ran al Qaeda leaders out of the country.

In a highly controversial move, the Bush administration next expanded the war on terror to invade Iraq, a country that administration officials suggested was linked to al Qaeda and the 9/11 attacks, and which they claimed was trying to develop weapons of mass destruction (chemical, biological, and nuclear weapons). On March 19, 2003, U.S. troops invaded Iraq and

Homeland Security Corruption

Federal budgets for domestic counterterrorism efforts increased by billions of dollars following the 9/11 terrorist attacks. These increased budgets attracted profiteers seeking to benefit from the nation's tragedy. A 2006 congressional report found that the Homeland Security Department's contract system is rife with waste, misspent funds, and abuse. Lawmakers say that since the department's creation in 2003, it has issued numerous contracts without using a competitive bidding process. Specifically, the report found that thirty-two Homeland Security Department contracts worth a total of $34 billion were marked by significant overcharges, wasteful spending, or mismanagement. Among the contracts criticized were deals for hiring airport screeners, inspecting airport luggage, detecting radiation at the nation's ports, securing the borders, and housing Hurricane Katrina evacuees. Investigations of these contracts revealed items such as contractor bills for luxury hotel rooms, products that malfunctioned, and federal officials who bought personal items with government credit cards. Despite this extravagant spending, however, the Government Accounting Office (GAO) found in 2007 that the agency had made little to no progress in most of its central goals, including the areas of emergency preparedness and response, science and technology, human capital management, and information technology management.

quickly overthrew the regime of Iraqi leader Saddam Hussein. The war in Iraq, however, was opposed by many people, both in the United States and around the world, because it was viewed as an unnecessary war of choice that had no connection to 9/11. Ultimately, these critics were proven accurate when no weapons of mass destruction (WMD) were ever found and political experts confirmed that Iraq had no involvement in 9/11.

Today, more than six years after the 2001 attack, hundreds of billions of dollars have been spent by the United States for military and reconstruction costs, and thousands of lives have been lost and destroyed, but U.S. troops are still fighting in both Iraq and Afghanistan with no end in sight. In Afghanistan, for example, more than 340 U.S. soldiers have been killed, and more than 1,000 injured. The brunt of the war has hit the Afghan people; reportedly, more than 12,000 Afghan troops and civilians have died, and more than 30,000 have been injured. The numbers killed and injured in Iraq are similarly shocking. As the *Los Angeles Times* reported in 2007:

> The decision to invade Iraq has . . . cost us dearly. More than 3,700 American soldiers have lost their lives on foreign sands. Another 27,000 have returned home with injuries, many of them life-altering. Tens of thousands of Iraqis have been killed or wounded and about 4 million forced to flee, half of them to uncertain foreign refuge. Their scars will mar the future as anger over the U.S. invasion and occupation of Iraq . . . breeds new enemies.[55]

The monetary cost of these ambitious operations has also been great. Since September 11, 2001, in fact, experts say the United States has spent about $400 billion for military operations, reconstruction, and other programs in Iraq and Afghanistan, and the administration has requested $189 billion for 2008. According to analysts, in fact, the amount spent by the United States for the war on terror is fast approaching the cost of the entire war in Vietnam. As reporter Renee Schoof writes, "The Iraq war's cost is approaching that of the 1964–1973 Vietnam War's estimated total of $518 billion, in 2007 dollars."[56]

Moreover, many terrorism experts say the military excursion into Iraq has only produced more terrorism. Following the U.S. invasion, an anti-American insurgency developed among Iraqis that soon attracted Islamic jihadists from throughout the region. Just as the mujahideen fought the Soviets in Afghanistan decades earlier, these jihadists now attack American soldiers and Iraqi civilians. Although the Bush administration denies that the war has increased terrorism and claims that fighting the jihadists in Iraq prevents them from coming to the United States, the U.S. government's own analysts have contradicted the administration's view. A 2006 National Intelligence Estimate called "Trends in Global Terrorism: Implications for the United States," for example, states: "The Iraq War has become the 'cause celebre' for jihadists, breeding a deep resentment of US involvement in the Muslim world and cultivating supporters for the global jihadist movement."[57] According to terrorism experts, the Iraq region now produces more suicide bombings than anywhere else on the globe.

Reduced Civil Liberties

Many commentators maintain, however, that the most worrisome consequence of modern terrorism is the threat posed to the individual freedoms and civil liberties that have historically been protected in the world's democracies. In the United States, for example, critics accuse the Bush administration of using the war on terror as an excuse to expand the powers of the president and executive branch, at the expense of essential democratic freedoms. This criticism is based on several administration initiatives that vastly expanded government's search, surveillance, and interrogation powers.

Almost immediately after the attacks, for example, President Bush proposed new legislation called the Patriot Act. This legislation, the president claimed, was "essential not only to pursuing and punishing terrorists, but also preventing more atrocities in the hands of the evil ones."[58] In the crisis atmosphere following 9/11, Congress passed the legislation quickly and with virtually no debate or opposition. In fact, the bill was introduced and passed by overwhelming majorities in both houses of Congress within just a few days of its introduction. The act was signed into law on October 26, 2001, less than two months after 9/11.

From the start, however, the Patriot Act was highly controversial because it greatly broadened the right of the FBI and police to conduct searches of all Americans' private property and information. Some sections of the act, for example, allowed police to secretly search private homes and property, while others permitted taps on people's phones and monitoring of their Internet communications. Still other sections of the new law authorized law enforcement to search a wide variety of personal records, including financial, library, travel, video rental, phone, medical, and church records.

The Patriot Act permitted many of these new searches to be conducted without any type of advance judicial warrant. In some cases, the government was required to obtain a warrant from a special, secret court set up under the Foreign Intelligence Surveillance Act (FISA). However, the government generally did not have to show that the person being targeted had committed a crime or even that the person was involved in terrorism, but only that the information sought was relevant to a government terrorism investigation. Many searches were also authorized to be conducted in secret, and the law prohibited persons or businesses affected by certain types of surveillance from ever revealing the fact that they had been asked to provide information to the government. In addition, the law created a new crime called "domestic terrorism," which allowed the deportation of anyone who associates, even unknowingly, with terrorists, and authorized the temporary detention of aliens without any prior showing or court ruling that the person is dangerous. The act even prohibited judicial challenges to most of the government's new powers, giving the FBI virtually unrestrained powers to conduct terrorism investigations.

Civil rights advocates claimed that the Patriot Act threatened individual freedoms vital to American democracy and was an invitation for government abuse of power. Groups such as the American Civil Liberties Union (ACLU), for example, complained that the act allowed FBI agents to investigate American citizens without probable cause and subjected organizations to

The Patriot Act authorizes law enforcement to, among other things, search a wide variety of personal records, including financial, library, travel, video rental, phone, medical, and church records. As a result, many people feel that the Patriot Act is unconstitutional and should be repealed.

harassment for protected political activities. The group brought lawsuits claiming the legislation violated Americans' sacred constitutional rights—such as privacy, freedom of speech, freedom from unreasonable searches, and due process. In 2004, two courts ruled parts of the Patriot Act unconstitutional. One court disapproved of a section of the act that made it a crime to give "expert advice or assistance" to groups designated as foreign terrorist organizations, finding it to be unconstitutionally vague. Another 2004 ruling struck down the FBI's use of National Security Letters (NSLs), which allowed for secret searches of Internet and telephone records without a judicial warrant.

Despite the criticism and court challenges, however, President Bush urged that the entire act be renewed in 2005, when parts of the law were set to expire. Bush claimed, "The Patriot Act has accomplished exactly what it was designed to do—it has protected American liberty, and saved American lives."[59] After a period of congressional review, the Patriot Act was reauthorized in 2006 with a few safeguards to protect civil liberties. Civil libertarians, however, continue to successfully claim that the law is constitutionally flawed. In September 2007, for example, two more federal court decisions on the Patriot Act were issued—the

A LOSS OF AMERICAN VALUES

"The price of this president's military and domestic overreach [since 9/11] has been highest in the loss of faith in America itself, in the values and institutions that have historically defined this nation." —*Los Angeles Times*, "What We've Lost," September 11, 2007.

www.latimes.com/news/opinion/la-ed-war11sep11,0,5040527.story?coll=la-opinion-leftrail.

first upholding the 2004 finding on NSLs and the second ruling that two other provisions of the act are unconstitutional because they allow search warrants to be issued without probable cause as required by the Fourth Amendment.

The Patriot Act was just one of the president's post 9/11 actions that created civil rights protests. In 2002 President Bush quietly authorized the National Security Agency (NSA)—a supersecret government intelligence agency charged with collecting information on foreigners—to spy on persons inside the United States without the court search warrants normally required for domestic spying. The president later argued the program was necessary to rapidly monitor the phone calls of U.S. residents who may have contact with terrorist groups, but critics charged that the program was unconstitutional. Despite these protests, in August 2007 Congress voted to uphold warrantless domestic surveillance with the passage of the Protect America Act. This legislation, which expires in 2008, allows the attorney general and the director of national intelligence (DNI) to authorize surveillance of international phone calls without a warrant from the FISA court. President Bush praised the act, stating, "This law gives our intelligence professionals this greater flexibility while closing a dangerous gap in our intelligence gathering activities that threatened to weaken our defenses."[60] The ACLU, however, calls it the "Police America Act," and says it "allows for massive, untargeted collection of international communications without court order or meaningful oversight by either Congress or the courts."[61]

Additional actions taken by the administration in the name of 9/11 included the detention of nearly five hundred terrorist suspects in a U.S. military base in Guantánamo, Cuba, without charging them with a crime. The suspects were labeled enemy combatants, a term usually reserved for enemy soldiers captured on a battlefield. The administration also defends certain interrogation techniques in terror investigations that some consider to be torture. Many experts saw these decisions as unconstitutional and a violation of the Geneva Conventions, international treaties that govern the treatment of prisoners of war.

Other democratic, western countries such as Britain, Germany, and France have implemented their own antiterrorist programs in recent years and have encountered similar criticisms. As Amnesty International, a human rights organization, has warned: "In the name of fighting 'international terrorism', governments have rushed to introduce draconian new measures that threaten the human rights of their own citizens."[62] Although these measures are viewed by many as necessary to combat the current trend of global jihad terrorism, some observers say the ultimate cost of fighting terrorism could be democracy itself.

THE FUTURE
OF TERRORISM

Despite the billions spent on counterterrorism, homeland security, and military actions in recent years, experts expect terrorism to be a prominent part of our future. One reason is that the same globalization forces that are making the world more connected economically are also helping to foster the spread of terrorism and making it harder to control and prevent. This risk of future terrorism is increased by other factors as well, including the continuing U.S. interests in the resources of the Middle East. The worst case scenario is that future terrorists may gain access to weapons of mass destruction (WMD)—chemical, biological, or nuclear technology—that could be used to inflict catastrophic damage.

Globalization and Terrorism

Terrorism has existed for hundreds of years because it has great appeal as a means for the weak and powerless to confront much stronger enemies or powerful governments. For these reasons alone, experts say terrorist tactics are likely to continue to be used in the future. Western powers such as the United States, however, face the biggest terrorism threat due largely to the growing global jihadist network. As a Future of Terrorism Task Force created by the U.S. Department of Homeland Security predicted in a January 2007 report, "There is every indication that the number and magnitude of attacks on the U.S., its interests and its allies will likely increase."[63]

According to terrorism analysts, however, today's terrorism is aided by certain developments that are unique to our contemporary times. One of the most significant of these forces is globalization—the increased mobility of people and goods throughout the world. Global trade has helped to spur development and prosperity both in the developed world and in many developing countries, but many poor countries have been left out of this prosperity. People in regions still suffering from great poverty and oppression, including many parts of the Muslim world, often feel disenchanted and alienated, and some experts think these conditions create fertile ground for extremist and terrorist groups to grow.

In addition, improvements in communications that have accompanied globalization have helped to increase the ability of terrorists to connect with like-minded supporters and build their terrorist networks. Today, terrorists operating in different countries can communicate, exchange information, rally their supporters, and plan terrorist attacks over the Internet. This helps to create a global community unrestricted by physical or

Improvements in communication methods in today's world allow terrorists to connect with one another no matter their location. Here, Osama bin Laden delivers a video message via the Arab TV station Al-Jazeera.

بن لادن : قاتلنا أمريكا لأننا أحرار ولأننا نريد إرجاع الحرية لأمتنا

حصاد اليوم

national boundaries, in which participants find their identity in extremist or fundamentalist ideologies rather than in the places they actually live. As terrorism experts Daniel Benjamin and Steven Simon conclude, "The Internet has accelerated the spread of everything from radical Islamist ideology to the minutiae of bomb making for a growing community of jihadists around the world."[64]

In fact, experts say that the number of Web sites promoting violence and exalting terrorism has exploded during the last decade. Gabriel Weimann of Haifa University in Israel, for example, claims that Web sites run by terrorist groups have grown from 12 in 1998 to about 4,400 today, and that does not include many other sites that are not officially associated with terrorist groups. A majority of these sites spread radical Islamist propaganda, in a wide variety of forms. As Benjamin and Simon explain:

> Chat rooms serve to establish personal contacts and provide space for views that are too extreme for posting to the site itself. To grab the attention of children, some sites present cartoons, interactive games, fables, adventure stories—as well as images of children playing with real weapons playacting as terrorists. For adolescents, there are rap videos. . . . For those a little older, there are applications for recruitment accompanied by background "investigation" forms, job listings, and links to stores where books and pamphlets that glamorize jihad can be bought.[65]

The jihadist Web sites also post daily videos showing terrorists, often those involved in the war in Iraq, shooting down enemy helicopters with shoulder-fired missiles, bombing American vehicles or buildings with improvised explosive devices (IEDs), or shooting American troops with assault rifles. By showing Muslim fighters dominating western forces, these images are designed to inspire, boost morale, and promote recruitment efforts of terrorist groups. Often, these images are mixed with others that show the death and suffering of Muslims and their children at the hands of foreign troops—a sight that further stokes feelings of retaliation and extremist jihad among supporters.

U.S. Interests in the Middle East

Another factor that may inspire future terrorist activity is a continuing U.S. presence or involvement in the Middle East—a likely scenario because the United States views the area as strategically important to its national interests. Today as in the past, ensuring a dependable supply of oil from the region is a key part of U.S. foreign policy. Mamoun Fandy of the Center for Contemporary Arab Studies at Georgetown University explains:

> Securing the flow of affordable oil is a cornerstone of U.S. Middle East policy. The U.S. strategy of dual containment of Iran and Iraq, designed to ensure that neither Iraq nor Iran is capable of threatening neighboring

The Islamic militant group Jihad burns a U.S. flag in protest over the continued presence of U.S. troops in the Middle East.

Gulf countries, is inextricably linked to Washington's oil policy. . . . Although only about 10% of oil used in the U.S. is imported from the region. . . . Gulf oil remains important because of its impact on the global economy. U.S. competitors in Europe and Japan depend much more on Gulf oil than the U.S. does: 30% of European oil imports and nearly 80% of Japan's come from the Gulf. The U.S. exerts significant influence on these countries through control of Gulf oil.[66]

In fact, many observers think ensuring access to Iraq's vast, untapped oil reserves is the real reason the United States invaded Iraq and is still fighting there today.

In the view of many political commentators, this quest for oil may bring ever more persistent U.S. activities and involve-

IRAQ'S ROLE IN THE WAR ON TERROR

"The Armed Forces of the United States are engaged in a struggle [in Iraq] that will determine the direction of the global war on terror—and our safety here at home." —George W. Bush, president of the United States.

George W. Bush, President's Address to the Nation, January 10, 2007. www.white house.gov/news/releases/2007/01/20070110-7.html.

ment in the Middle East region in years to come. This is because world oil reserves are believed to be peaking, either now or in the near future. After the peak, experts say, oil and natural gas will be harder to extract and supplies and output will decline year after year, forcing countries to compete for dwindling supplies of oil. Even worse, this decline in energy supplies comes when the world's demand for fossil fuel energy is skyrocketing due to rapid economic development in countries such as China and India. Since about one-quarter of the world's oil is found in the Middle East, most observers predict that the United States will continue to assert its influence in the area.

This U.S. involvement in the center of the Muslim world, however, is the main grievance asserted by jihadist groups such

Terrorists can use internet cafes across the globe to communicate and plan without fear of identification.

as al Qaeda. For example, on February 23, 1998, when al Qaeda first called for a jihad against the United States, Osama bin Laden urged Muslims to kill the Americans and their allies in order to force U.S. soldiers "out of all the lands of Islam."[67] Most observers, therefore, believe the stage is set for a continuing, and possibly escalating, battle of wills between the jihadists and American policy makers—a situation that will likely be a recipe for more, not less, terrorism.

The Increasing Capabilities of Terrorists

Terrorism is also likely to flourish in the future because of the proven resiliency of contemporary terrorists. Experts say today's terrorists learn from other terrorist groups and are highly adaptive, making them ever more dangerous. As the Web site Terrorism Research explains: "Terrorism continues to adapt to . . . [counterterrorism measures] and exploit developments in technology and society. . . . Terrorists are developing new capabilities of attack and improving the efficiency of existing methods. Additionally, terrorist groups . . . [are] becoming prominent as international influences in their own right."[68]

The global jihadist network, for example, has responded to the U.S. war on terror by becoming highly decentralized, with no one operational leader and instead a large number of smaller groups that operate relatively independently. This decentralization helps al Qaeda weather disruptions caused by the killing or imprisonment of key leaders, and makes it harder for governments to attack the organization or predict the location or nature of its attacks. Al Qaeda terrorists in Iraq have also been quick to adapt their bombing and weapons techniques to each new U.S. defense, and have employed new technology, such as disposable cell phones and Internet cafés, in their operations and communications around the world. As a result of these adaptations, the jihadists are becoming increasingly sophisticated, efficient, and capable, as well as more lethal.

Chemical and Biological Weapons

Although nuclear weapons would be the most destructive of all weapons of mass destruction (WMD), terrorists could also do great damage with chemical or biological weapons. An attack using some type of chemical nerve gas such as the mustard gas used in World War II, if released in a confined urban setting, could also kill hundreds or thousands, although the contamination left behind might not be capable of destroying whole cities. Similarly, biological weapons such as a vaccine-resistant smallpox or other type of virus could easily set off an epidemic of disease that could potentially kill thousands. Like nuclear weapons, these types of WMD are more available today than in the past. Although most governments possessing stocks of these weapons have promised to destroy them, some stocks still remain. Russia is the largest storehouse of both chemical and biological weapons, and its lax security and problem with organized crime has caused many experts to worry that toxic agents could fall into the hands of dangerous terrorist groups.

Terrorists with Weapons of Mass Destruction

The world's biggest fear, however, is that fanatical terrorists may one day gain access to weapons of mass destruction (WMD)—that is, nuclear, biological, or chemical weapons. As terrorism expert Walter Laqueur explains,

> [Terrorism] has become one of the gravest dangers facing mankind. For the first time in history, weapons of enormous destructive power are both readily acquired and harder to track. Science and technology have made enormous progress, but human nature, alas, has not changed. There is as much fanaticism and madness as there ever was, and there are now very powerful weapons of mass destruction available to the terrorist. . . . In the near future it will be technologically possible to kill thousands, perhaps hundreds of thousands, not to mention the toll the panic that is likely to ensue may take. In brief, there has been a radical transformation, if not a revolution, in the character of terrorism, a fact we are still reluctant to accept.[69]

Terrorism expert Jessica Stern says that there are several developments that increase the risk that terrorists will use WMD. First, such weapons are valuable to modern religious terrorists whose goals include wanting to kill large numbers of people and who appear to be more likely to commit acts of extreme violence. Also, Stern notes that since the breakup of the Soviet Union at the end of the 1980s, WMD and information about how to use them are readily available in the underground markets. Indeed, even some governments, such as North Korea, are believed to be exporting WMD materials for profit. Finally, Stern says, advances in weapons and communications technology have made WMD terrorism easier to carry out.

The costs of such a WMD attack, particularly a nuclear attack, are almost unfathomable. A study by Harvard University, for example, tried to determine the economic costs of a ten-kiloton bomb set off at New York's Grand Central Station and found that they would be "staggering"[70]—at least several trillion dollars. The cost of lost salaries of those killed, the study found, would be at least $1 trillion; the cost of treating the wounded would be hundreds of billions more; and the list of costs goes on to include massive destruction of property and infrastructure, unknown economic output losses, and huge decontamination costs. Other lives would likely be lost as people around the country panic, and residual radioactivity would continue to cause health problems for years into the future. And if more than one city were hit, the mounting losses could even severely wound the national economy, dramatically lower Americans' standard of living, and diminish the United States as a world power.

However, some analysts point out that terrorists may not need to resort to WMD to carry out spectacular and high-casualty attacks. As Benjamin and Simon explain, the easiest option "is to use 'conventional' means—for the most part, available explosives—to strike targets whose destruction will cause mass casualties and, potentially, far-reaching economic disruption."[71] After all, the 9/11 terrorists simply used jet planes to create massive destruction. U.S. chemical plants or vehicles that carry chemicals could also be targeted, causing toxic fumes to spread and endanger millions of people. Another non-WMD option is basic explosives packed with a small amount of radioactive materials—a "dirty bomb"—which could release radioactivity over a huge area. If used in a large urban center such as New York, the human carnage and economic damage would be smaller than a nuclear bomb attack, but still unthinkable.

The Cyberterrorism Threat

Another type of potential terrorist threat predicted to emerge in the future is cyberterrorism—attacks on a country's computer systems. Because of rapid technological developments, many industries, businesses, and governments are increasingly dependent on computers and electronic communications, making them highly vulnerable. This is especially true in highly developed countries such as the United States. By disrupting these computers through computer viruses, worms, or other sabotage methods, terrorists could create havoc in key sectors of the economy such as banking or telecommunications, shut down

The 9/11 Commission Report

Following the terrorist attacks on September 11, 2001, the United States created the National Commission on Terrorist Attacks Upon the United States (often called the "9/11 Commission") to investigate the causes of the attack and make recommendations to policy makers. The commission's final report, released on July 22, 2004, identified numerous intelligence failures made by the Federal Bureau of Investigation (FBI) and the Central Intelligence Agency (CIA) that contributed to the nation's failure to prevent the 9/11 attacks. The commission also made several recommendations for improving the United States' antiterrorism efforts, some of which were later enacted. The commissioners in 2005 issued a report card on the progress made, concluding that the country was safer from terrorism, but not safe enough. Two years later, in 2007, two members of the 9/11 commission argued that the United States still lacked a sense of urgency needed to prevent another terrorist attack. In an article published on September 9, 2007, in the *Washington Post*, former governor of New Jersey Thomas H. Kean and former U.S. congressman Lee H. Hamilton said the country's progress on detecting, preventing, and responding to terrorist attacks has been "difficult, incomplete and slow" and that the nation faces a "rising tide of radicalization and rage in the Muslim world."

Thomas H. Kean and Lee H. Hamilton, "Are We Safer Today?" *The Washington Post*, September 9, 2007, p. B01. www.washingtonpost.com/wp-dyn/content/article /2007/09/07/AR2007090702050_pf.html.

vital utilities or air traffic control systems, or even disrupt a country's national defense systems.

Although many experts have downplayed the threat of cyberterrorism and noted that no major instances of cyberterror have yet occurred, others believe it is a growing danger. High-tech hackers (not linked to terrorist groups) have already shown that such computer break-ins are possible. In February 2000, for example, the Web sites of several well-known American companies, including Amazon.com, eBay, and Yahoo, were attacked and shut down for several hours by hackers. And on October 22, 2002, hackers attacked the very heart of the Internet—thirteen "root servers" that provide the main pathways for almost all Internet communications worldwide. This attack caused little damage because of safeguards in the system, but future attacks might well be more successful.

Today, in fact, it is possible to find Internet Web sites devoted to "e-jihad"—a term used to describe Islamic cyberterrorism. Experts say jihadist terrorists clearly have a desire to improve their cyber skills and pursue this form of terrorism, so it may just be a matter of time before such attacks become more common.

Solutions Difficult

Despite the predictions about the future and the significant resources that have been directed at the problem already, experts remain divided over the best strategies for combating terrorism. To date, various counterterrorism methods have been used with vary-

As of 2008, the U.S. government has argued that U.S. troops must remain in Iraq in order to prevent the terrorists from attacking Americans at home.

ing rates of success. Before 9/11, for example, many countries saw terrorism as a criminal justice matter and fought it with law enforcement tools. In the United States, the Federal Bureau of Investigation (FBI)—the investigative arm of the U.S. Justice Department—was charged with preventing and prosecuting terrorism in the United States. This system prosecuted several major international terrorism cases, including al Qaeda's 1993 bombing of the World Trade Center and its 1998 bombings of U.S. embassies in Nairobi, Kenya, and Dar es Salaam, Tanzania. Other defendants were convicted for plotting terrorist attacks that were never carried out.

AMERICA IS LOSING THE WAR ON TERROR

"It is simply no longer possible to maintain that the United States is winning the war on terror. The number of terrorists is growing, as is the pool of people who may be moved to violence, and the means and know-how for carrying out attacks, including catastrophic ones, are becoming more readily available." —Daniel Benjamin, a senior fellow at the Center for Strategic and International Studies, a public policy think tank, and Steven Simon, a professor at Georgetown University.

Daniel Benjamin and Steven Simon, *The Next Attack*. New York: Times Books, 2005, p. 126.

After 9/11, however, the United States and some other countries began to see terrorism, particularly jihadist terrorism, as more of an international threat. This realization that terrorism is a global phenomenon caused the United States to shift toward a military strategy against al Qaeda and brought U.S. and some British forces into the current conflicts in Afghanistan and Iraq. Since then, U.S. president George W. Bush has consistently argued that the U.S. troops must remain in Iraq in order to prevent the terrorists from attacking Americans at home. As Bush explained in August 2004: "An immediate withdrawal of our troops in Iraq, or the broader Middle East, as some have called for, would only embolden the terrorists and create a staging ground to launch more attacks against America and free nations.

So long as I'm the President, we will stay, we will fight, and we will win the war on terror."[72]

Supporters of President Bush's military approach claim that it has succeeded in preventing another terrorist attack in the United States by disrupting critical terrorist operations and killing or capturing many senior al Qaeda members whose skills and experience have not been replaced. As one former senior U.S. intelligence official anonymously explained to reporters, "If the question is why al Qaeda hasn't carried out another 9/11 attack, the answer I think is that if they could have, they would have."[73] Other analysts say that the U.S. invasions of Afghanistan and Iraq have only strengthened al Qaeda and created more terrorism. Former government terrorism expert Richard A. Clarke, for example, testified in 2004, "There have been more major al Qaeda related attacks globally in the 30 months since 9-11 than there were in the 30 months preceding it. Hostility toward the

How Do We Fight a War Against a Tactic?

"To declare war on [terrorism, which] . . . is, after all, a tactic does not appear to make a great deal of sense." —Louise Richardson, executive dean of the Radcliffe Institute for Advanced Study, a senior lecturer in government at Harvard University, and a lecturer on law at Harvard Law School.

Louise Richardson, *What Terrorists Want*. New York: Random House, 2006, p. 63.

US in the Islamic world has increased since 9-11, largely as a result of the invasion and occupation of Iraq."[74] And other analysts say the continuing presence of western troops in Iraq helps draw more terrorists into al Qaeda's organization. As reporter Andrew Tilghman put it in a 2007 article, "The continued American occupation of Iraq is al-Qaeda's best recruitment tool, the lure to hook new recruits."[75]

Indeed, some commentators have said that al Qaeda is quite pleased with the results of its jihadist campaign so far and plans to expand it in the future. Jordanian journalist Fouad Hussein, who has spoken with some members of al Qaeda's inner circle, has said that the group's plan has seven phases, and that the aim of phase one—and 9/11—was to awaken Muslims by provoking the United States to declare war on Islam. "The first phase," Hussein explains, "was judged by the strategists and masterminds behind al-Qaida as very successful."[76] Phase two is a recruitment phase, centered in Iraq, followed by phase three

NO GUARANTEES OF SAFETY

"Despite the advances in countering terrorism it must always be recognized that it is . . . impossible to guarantee personal and collective security from . . . terrorism." —Stephen Sloan, professor and fellow in the Global Perspectives Office at the University of Central Florida.

Stephen Sloan, *Terrorism: The Present Threat in Context*. New York: Berg, 2006, p. 101.

attacks on Israel and Turkey to increase al Qaeda's support. Next, according to Hussein, al Qaeda plans phase four, which will include attacks on Mideast oil facilities to destabilize secular Arab governments and cyberattacks to target the U.S. economy. By phase five, al Qaeda hopes to have weakened western influence enough so that it can declare an Islamic state in the Middle East, and the last two phases are expected to include a period of total war between Islamic forces and nonbelievers capped by an Islamic victory and successful Islamic rule.

Military action, however, does not rule out the simultaneous use of other tactics, and a number of other strategies are also being implemented to stop terrorists. The United States and many other countries have beefed up their intelligence and surveillance efforts—programs that monitor communications, infiltrate terrorist organizations, and try to thwart terror plots before they are implemented. Financial strategies, too, are used to track and freeze monetary donations and support of terrorist organizations. Diplomacy and political cooperation with other countries is also critical, according to many experts, as is propaganda aimed at discrediting extremist ideologies and religions.

In an age of international terrorism, countries can also work together to share information, coordinate operations to kill or capture terrorists, and control the global distribution of WMD that might fall into the hands of terrorists. Ultimately, most experts seem to agree that no one strategy is a magic bullet that will end terrorism; instead, there appears to be a variety of options, all of which will be important in what is expected to be a long global struggle. As FBI director Robert Mueller has said, "The struggle against terrorism . . . may persist for generations."[77]

At the same time, it is important for individuals to remember that the actual threat of terrorism is quite low for the average person; some experts say close to zero. Researchers note, for example, that car crashes in developed countries such as the United States kill almost four hundred times more people than terrorist attacks. Since 9/11, the government and the media have bombarded the public with messages about the need to fear terrorism, but psychologists say people should go about their lives and not worry excessively about being personally affected by terrorism. As political scientist Ben Friedman explains, "Conventional wisdom says that none of us are safe from terrorism. The truth is that almost all of us are."[78]

Introduction: The New U.S. Enemy

1. BBC News, "Bush Likens War on Terrorism to Cold War," *ABC News Online*, May 28, 2006. www.abc.net.au/news/newsitems/ 200605/s1649115.htm.
2. Quoted in William Greider, "Under the Banner of the 'War' on Terror," *Nation,* June 3, 2004. www.thenation.com/doc/2004 0621/greider.

Chapter 1: Defining Terrorism

3. Walter Laqueur, *The New Terrorism: Fanaticism and the Arms of Mass Destruction*. New York: Oxford University Press, 1999, p. 6.
4. Quoted in Laqueur, *The New Terrorism*, p. 5.
5. Title 22 of the U.S. Code, Section 2656f(d).
6. National Counterterrorism Center, "A Chronology of Significant International Terrorism for 2004," April 25, 2005, p. vii. www. fas.org/irp/threat/nctc2004.pdf.
7. Quoted in Carroll Payne, "Understanding Terrorism—Definition of Terrorism," *World Conflict Quarterly*, May 2007. www.global terrorism101.com/UTDefinition.html.
8. The White House, "The National Security Strategy of the United States of America," September 2002. www.whitehouse.gov/nsc/ nss3.html.
9. Title 18 of the U.S. Code, Section 2331.
10. Title 28 of the U.S. Code of Federal Regulations, Section 0.85.
11. Quoted in United Nations Office on Crime and Drugs, "Definitions of Terrorism," 2006. www.unodc.org/unodc/terrorism_defi nitions.html.
12. Quoted in United Nations Office on Crime and Drugs, "Definitions of Terrorism."
13. Quoted in United Nations Office on Crime and Drugs, "Definitions of Terrorism."
14. Quoted in Payne, "Understanding Terrorism."

15. Bruce Hoffman, *Inside Terrorism*. New York: Columbia University Press, 1998, p. 15.

16. Quoted in Hoffman, *Inside Terrorism*, p. 16.

17. Quoted in Laqeur, *The New Terrorism*, p. 23.

18. Quoted in Hoffman, *Inside Terrorism*, p. 26.

Chapter 2: The Current Threat: Islamic Terrorism

19. Monte Palmer and Princess Palmer, *At the Heart of Terror*. New York: Rowman & Littlefield, 2004, p. 1.

20. Louise Richardson, *What Terrorists Want*. New York: Random House, 2006, p. 61.

21. Richardson, *What Terrorists Want*, p. 65.

22. Palmer and Palmer, *At the Heart of Terror*, p. 99.

23. Palmer and Palmer, *At the Heart of Terror*, p. 117.

24. Lionel Beehner, "Al-Qaeda in Iraq: Resurging or Splintering?" Council on Foreign Relations, July 16, 2007. www.cfr.org/publication/13007/alqaeda_in_iraq.html.

25. Quoted in The White House, "Setting the Record Straight: Iraq Is the Central Front of Al Qaeda's Global Campaign," May 3, 2007. www.whitehouse.gov/news/releases/2007/05/20070503-6.html.

26. Bruce-Riedel, "Al Qaeda Strikes Back," *Foreign Affairs*, May/June 2007. www.foreignaffairs.org/20070501faessay86304-p0/bruce-riedel/al-qaeda-strikes-back.html.

27. Quoted in Riedel, "Al Qaeda Strikes Back."

Chapter 3: Motivations, Tactics, and Targets

28. George W. Bush, Address to a Joint Session of Congress and the American People, September 20, 2001. www.whitehouse.gov/news/releases/2001/09/20010920-8.html.

29. Quoted in BBC News, "Wrong to Call Terrorists 'Madmen,'" July 9, 2004. http://news.bbc.co.uk/2/hi/health/3880777.stm.

30. Terry McDermott, *Perfect Soldiers*. New York: HarperCollins, 2005, p. xvi.

31. McDermott, *Perfect Soldiers*, p. xvi.

32. Stephen Sloan, *Terrorism: The Present Threat in Context*. New York: Berg, 2006, p. 20.

33. Sloan, *Terrorism*, p. 21.

34. Richardson, *What Terrorists Want*, pp. 43–44.

35. Hoffman, *Inside Terrorism*, p. 43.
36. Quoted in Richardson, *What Terrorists Want*, p. 42.
37. Richardson, *What Terrorists Want*, p. 90.
38. Quoted in Richardson, *What Terrorists Want*, p. 43.
39. Jessica Stern, *Terror in the Name of God*. New York: HarperCollins, 2003, p. 282.
40. Stern, *Terror in the Name of God*, p. 285.
41. Hoffman, *Inside Terrorism*, p. 43.
42. Hoffman, *Inside Terrorism*, p. 183.
43. Robert Pape, *Dying to Win: The Strategic Logic of Suicide Terrorism*. New York: Random House, 2005, p. 4.
44. Pape, *Dying to Win*, p. 79.
45. Pape, *Dying to Win*, p. 80.
46. Pape, *Dying to Win*, p. 104.
47. Marc Sageman, *Understanding Terror Networks*. Philadelphia: University of Pennsylvania Press, 2004, p. 1.
48. Palmer and Palmer, *At the Heart of Terror*, pp. 129–130.
49. Hoffman, *Inside Terrorism*, p. 93.
50. Hoffman, *Inside Terrorism*, p. 94.
51. Brian Martin, "Terrorism: Ethics, Effectiveness and Enemies," *Social Alternatives*, 2004, Vol. 23, No. 2, pp. 36–37. www.uow.edu.au/arts/sts/bmartin/pubs/04sa.html.

Chapter 4: Terrorism's High Costs

52. Robert Looney, "Economic Costs to the United States Stemming from the 9/11 Attacks," *Strategic Insights*, August 2002, Vol. I, Iss. 6. http://www.ccc.nps.navy.mil/si/aug02/homeland.asp.
53. Dick K. Nanto, "9/11 Terrorism: Global Economic Costs," *Congressional Research Service*, October 4, 2004, p. 3. http://digital.library.unt.edu/govdocs/crs/permalink/meta-crs-7725:1.
54. Angie C. Marek, "Security At Any Price? Homeland Protection Isn't Just Job 1 in Washington; It's More Like a Big Old Government ATM," *US News & World Report*, May 22, 2005. www.usnews.com/usnews/news/articles/050530/30homeland.htm.
55. *Los Angeles Times*, "What We've Lost," September 11, 2007. www.latimes.com/news/opinion/la-ed-war11sep11,0,5040527.story?coll=la-opinion-leftrail.
56. Renee Schoof, "$42 Billion More Requested for Iraq, Afghanistan

Wars," *MCT News Service, San Diego Union-Tribune*, September 27, 2007, p. A-13.

57. Director of National Intelligence, "Declassified Key Judgments of the National Intelligence Estimate 'Trends in Global Terrorism: Implications for the United States,'" April 2006. www.dni.gov/press_releases/Declassified_NIE_Key_Judgments.pdf.

58. George W. Bush, Remarks at the Signing of the Patriot Act, October 26, 2001.

59. George W. Bush, Speech at the Ohio State Highway Patrol Academy in Columbus, Ohio, June 9, 2005. www.whitehouse.gov/news/releases/2005/06/20050609-2.html.

60. Quoted in Nathan Burchfiel, "FISA Expansion Sparks Civil Liberties Concerns," CNSNews.com, August 7, 2007. www.cnsnews.com/ViewPolitics.asp?Page=/Politics/archive/200708/POL20070807a.html.

61. ACLU, "ACLU Fact Sheet on 'Police America Act,'" 2007. www.aclu.org/safefree/nsaspying/31203res20070807.html.

62. Amnesty International, "The Backlash: Human Rights at Risk Around the World," October 4, 2001. http://web.amnesty.org/library/index/engACT300272001?OpenDocument.

Chapter 5: The Future of Terrorism

63. Homeland Security Advisory Council Future of Terrorism Task Force, Report, January 2007, p. 3. http://72.14.253.104/search?q=cache:jK7F-RUr2AsJ:www.dhs.gov/xlibrary/assets/hsac-future-terrorism-010107.pdf+future+of+terrorism&hl=en&ct=clnk&cd=2&gl=us.

64. Daniel Benjamin and Steven Simon, *The Next Attack*. New York: Times Books, 2005, p. xvii.

65. Benjamin and Simon, *The Next Attack*, pp. 60–61.

66. Mamoun Fandy, "U.S. Oil Policy in the Middle East," *Foreign Policy in Focus*, January 1997, Vol. 2, No. 4. http://www.fpif.org/briefs/vol2/v2n4oil_body.html.

67. Quoted in Gar Smith, "Defeat Terrorism: Abandon Oil," *Earth Island Journal*, Spring 2002. www.thirdworldtraveler.com/Sept_11_2001/Abandon_Oil.html.

68. Terrorism Research, "Future Trends in Terrorism," undated. www.terrorism-research.com/future/.

69. Laqueur, *The New Terrorism*, p. 4.

70. Quoted in Joshua S. Goldstein, *The Real Cost of War: How You Pay for the War on Terror*. New York: New York University Press, 2004, p. 136.

71. Benjamin and Simon, *The Next Attack*, p. 130.

72. George W. Bush, Speech to military families in Nampa, Idaho, August 24, 2005. www.whitehouse.gov/news/releases/2005/08/20050824.html.

73. Quoted in David Morgan, "Bush Success vs. Al Qaeda Breeds Future Worries," Reuters, April 3, 2007. http://uk.reuters.com/article/worldNews/idUKN3025663920070403.

74. Quoted in Mia Bloom, *Dying to Kill: The Allure of Suicide Terror*. New York: Columbia University Press, p. 182.

75. Andrew Tilghman, "The Myth of AQI," *Washington Monthly*, October 2007. www.washingtonmonthly.com/features/2007/0710.tilghman.html.

76. Quoted in Yassin Musharbash, "What al-Qaida Really Wants," *Speigel Online International*, August 12, 2005. www.spiegel.de/international/0,1518,369448,00.html.

77. Robert Mueller, Prepared remarks, September 28, 2007. www.cfr.org/publication/14323/prepared_remarks_by_the_fbis_robert_mueller.html?breadcrumb=%2Fissue%2F135%2Fterrorism.

78. Ben Friedman, "The Real Cost of Homeland Security," *AlterNet*, February 9, 2006. www.alternet.org/audits/31514/.

Chapter 1: Defining Terrorism

1. What are some of the common factors in the various definitions of terrorism?
2. Give two examples of what some experts call state terrorism, one from history and one from the modern world.
3. Give two examples of terrorism in which the terrorist group fought or is fighting for a revolutionary or nationalist cause, one from history and one from the modern world.

Chapter 2: The Current Threat: Islamic Terrorism

1. Explain the meaning of the word jihad, as it is used by Islamic terrorist groups.
2. Name the three contemporary political events that helped to inspire the growth of radical Islam and jihadist terrorism.
3. In what locations has al Qaeda carried out successful terrorist attacks since its 9/11 attacks on the United States?

Chapter 3: Motivations, Tactics, and Targets

1. According to experts quoted in the book, how do most individual terrorists tend to see themselves?
2. What are some of the motivations of terrorist groups, according to the experts quoted in the book?
3. Describe some practical reasons for the use of terrorist tactics.

Chapter 4: Terrorism's High Costs

1. How many people were killed in the 9/11 terrorist attacks? What types of injuries resulted from the attacks?
2. What military actions has the United States taken in its "war on terror?"

3. What are some of the objections to the Patriot Act, according to the author?

Chapter 5: The Future of Terrorism

1. How has globalization affected terrorism, according to the author?

2. How is the U.S. reliance on oil as an energy source related to jihadist terrorism, according to many commentators?

3. After reading this book, do you think the threat of terrorism is high or low for most Americans? Explain the reasons for your answer.

GLOSSARY

al Qaeda: An Islamic group formed by Osama bin Laden that has carried out attacks against Americans and others, including the September 11, 2001, World Trade Center attack.

al Qaeda in Iraq (AQI): A branch of al Qaeda located in Iraq and led by Abu Ayyub al-Masri, an Egyptian.

apartheid: An official policy of racial segregation against black South Africans practiced in the Republic of South Africa from 1948 until the early 1990s.

Chechens: An Islamic ethnic group that has fought since the early 1990s for independence from Russia.

civil liberties: The freedoms that protect individual citizens from arbitrary or oppressive government action.

counterterrorism: Efforts to prevent, reduce, or stop terrorist violence.

freedom fighter: A term used to describe someone who fights for political independence or change.

Front de Liberation Nationale (FLN): A Muslim resistance group that fought for Algeria's independence from French colonial rule in the 1950s.

fundamentalist: A term that usually refers to someone who follows a strict, conservative version of a religion that seeks to apply the fundamental truths of their faith.

Great Purge: A campaign of repression and state-run terror carried out by Joseph Stalin, a leader of the former Soviet Union, in the 1930s, to eliminate all threats to his rule.

guerrilla warfare: A term that refers to military operations conducted by irregular, nongovernmental fighters using unconventional methods and tactics.

gulag: An inhumane prison system in the former Soviet Union during the leadership of Joseph Stalin in the 1930s.

Harakat ul-Mujahideen (HuM): An Islamic group in Pakistan that seeks Islamic rule.

Hezbollah: An Iranian-supported Islamic group based in Lebanon that has conducted terrorist attacks on Israel and other targets.

Hutus and Tutsis: Two tribes in Rwanda; governing Hutus have waged a campaign to kill Tutsis and some Hutus in the mid-1990s.

Irgun: A Jewish group that fought in the 1940s to end British rule in Palestinian regions and to create an independent Jewish state.

Irish Republican Army (IRA): A group that fought against British rule in Northern Ireland beginning in the 1920s.

Islamic Jihad: An Islamic group founded in Egypt, with a Palestinian branch that opposes Israel and seeks to create Islamic governments in the Middle East.

Islamist: A term usually used to refer to Muslims who follow a fundamentalist, or strict, version of Islam.

Janjaweed: Arab militias funded by the government of Sudan that have attacked and killed many of the country's black population since 1989.

jihad: An Arabic word that means "striving in the way of God." It can mean simply trying to be a better person, but it is often used to refer to a war fought in defense of Islam.

Kurdistan Workers Party (PKK): An ethnic group based in Turkey that is fighting to create an independent socialist Kurdish state of Kurdistan that would cover parts of Turkey, Iraq, Syria, and Iran.

Lashkar-e-Toiba (LT): An Islamic group in Pakistan that seeks Islamic rule.

Liberation Tigers of Tamil Eelam (LTTE or "Tamil Tigers"): A group formed by the Tamils, an ethnic group in Sri Lanka, to fight for political independence from that country's majority ethnic group, the Sinhalese.

mujahideen: An army of fundamentalist Islamic militants who fought to oust the Soviets from Afghanistan in the 1980s.

Muslim Brotherhood: A group founded in Egypt dedicated to promoting Islamic fundamentalism.

narcoterrorism: A form of terrorism that is linked with selling drugs and other crimes.

Palestine Liberation Organization (PLO): An organization founded in 1964 to free Palestinians from Israel's occupation of areas earlier occupied by Arabs.

"propaganda of the deed": A term that refers to the publicity and media attention generated by a violent attack or act.

sect: A subdivision or smaller part of a larger religious or ethnic group.

secular: A term that means not concerned with or connected to religion.

sharia: Islamic religious law.

Shia (Shiite): One of two sects within Islam that accounts for about 10 to 15 percent of the world's Muslim population.

state terrorism: Acts of repression and violence committed by a government or government leader against the country's citizens.

Stern Gang: A Jewish group that fought in the 1940s to end British rule in Palestinian regions and to create an independent Jewish state.

strategy vs. tactic: A strategy is the overall plan of action, while the term tactic refers to specific details, a part, or the means of carrying out the larger strategy.

Sunni: One of two sects within Islam that makes up the majority of the world's Muslim population.

Tabligi Jamaat: A religious organization in Pakistan that promotes Islamic fundamentalism.

Taliban: A fundamentalist Muslim group that ruled Afghanistan from 1996 until 2001 and that was friendly with al Qaeda.

Wahhabism: A particular brand of fundamentalist Islam that developed in Saudi Arabia and follows the teachings of Arab theologian Muhammad ibn 'Abd al-Wahhab at-Tamimi.

WMD: Weapons of mass destruction, including nuclear, chemical, and biological weapons.

ORGANIZATIONS TO CONTACT

American Civil Liberties Union (ACLU)
125 Broad Street, 18th Floor
New York, NY 10004
Ph: (212) 549-2585
Fax: (212) 549-2646
Web site: www.aclu.org

The American Civil Liberties Union (ACLU) is a nonprofit and non-partisan organization that works to preserve the protections and guarantees contained in the Bill of Rights to the U.S. Constitution, including the First Amendment rights to free speech, association, assembly, and religion; the right to a free press; the right to due process of law; and the right to privacy. The ACLU has been very active in opposing the Patriot Act, and its Web site contains a wealth of information about the act and its implementation as part of the war on terror.

Center for Advanced Studies on Terrorism (CAST)
1901 Avenue of the Stars, Suite 1555
Los Angeles, CA 90067
Ph: (310) 286-7485
Fax: (310) 286-7486
E-mail: info@terrorstudies.org
Web site: www.terrorstudies.org/

The Center for Advanced Studies on Terrorism (CAST) is an independent nonprofit institute dedicated to research on terrorism and the development of effective strategies for meeting the terrorist threat and other key national security issues. Its Web site lists publications and links related to terrorism.

Center for Constitutional Rights (CCR)
666 Broadway, 7th Floor
New York, NY 10012
Ph: (212) 614-6464

Fax: (212) 614-6499
Web site: www.ccr-ny.org/v2/home.asp

The Center for Constitutional Rights (CCR) is a nonprofit legal and educational organization dedicated to protecting and advancing the rights guaranteed by the U.S. Constitution and the United Nations' Universal Declaration of Human Rights. The group uses litigation proactively to defend civil and human rights and has been involved in litigation challenging the Patriot Act. A search on its Web site produces a number of publications relating to the Patriot Act.

Center for Strategic and International Studies (CSIS)
1800 K Street NW
Washington, DC 20006
Ph: (202) 887-0200
Fax: (202) 775-3199
Web site: www.csis.org

The Center for Strategic and International Studies (CSIS) is a nonprofit organization that seeks to advance global security and prosperity by conducting research and analysis and developing policy initiatives for decision makers. One area of focus for CSIS is terrorism, and its Web site contains a long list of publications on the subject, including reports written by experts, press articles, and congressional testimony.

Council on Foreign Relations
1779 Massachusetts Avenue NW
Washington, DC 20036
Ph: (202) 518-3400
Fax: (202) 986-2984
E-mail: knash@cfr.org
Web site: www.cfr.org/

The Council on Foreign Relations is an independent, nonpartisan membership organization, think tank, and publisher dedicated to being a resource for government, business, and the public on foreign policy issues facing the United States and other countries. Its Web site offers a wealth of information about the various types of terrorism (including suicide bombings), terrorist groups worldwide, and the U.S. responses following the September 11, 2001, attacks.

Institute for Counter-Terrorism (ICT)
Interdisciplinary Center (IDC)
P.O. Box 167
Herzliya 46150, Israel
Ph: 972-9-9527277
Fax: 972-9-9513073
Web site: www.ict.org.il

The International Policy Institute for Counter-Terrorism (ICT) is an academic institute and think tank for counterterrorism issues. Its mission is to facilitate international cooperation in the global struggle against terrorism and provide expertise to scholars and governments on terrorism, counterterrorism, homeland security, threat vulnerability and risk assessment, intelligence analysis, national security, and defense policy. Numerous reports are featured on ICT's Web site, many of them related to Palestinian terrorism.

RAND Corporation
1776 Main Street
Santa Monica, CA 90401-3208
Ph: (310) 393-0411
Fax: (310) 393-4818
Web site: www.rand.org/

The RAND Corporation is a nonprofit, public policy think tank that conducts research on important issues of national security, business, education, health, law, and science. One of RAND's research areas is terrorism and homeland security, and the group's Web site provides access to numerous reports, articles, testimony, and news commentary on this issue.

Terrorism Research Center
Ph: (877) 635-0816
Web site: www.terrorism.com/

The Terrorism Research Center (TRC) is an independent institute dedicated to the research of terrorism, information warfare, critical infrastructure protection, homeland security, and other issues of low-intensity political violence and gray-area phenomena. The group's Web site contains comprehensive information about terrorist groups, countries affected, intelligence reports, and other materials relating to the terrorist threat.

Books

Mary Habeck, *Knowing the Enemy: Jihadist Ideology and the War on Terror*. New Haven, CT: Yale University Press, 2006. A clear analysis of jihadism and the effectiveness of the war on terror.

Fiona Macdonald, *The September 11th Terrorist Attacks*. Milwaukee: World Almanac Library, 2004. A young adult book that describes the causes, events, people, and legacy of the September 11 terrorist attacks.

Phillip Margulies, *Al Qaeda: Osama bin Laden's Army of Terrorists*. New York: Rosen Publishing Group, 2003. Written for young adults, an overview of the Islamic terrorist group, al Qaeda, and its role in the September 11 terrorist attacks in the United States.

Matthew May, James L. Outman, and Elisabeth M. Outman, eds. *Terrorism Reference Library*. Detroit: UXL, 2003. In four volumes, offers young readers a wealth of information on global terrorism.

Malcolm Nance, *The Terrorists of Iraq: Inside the Strategy and Tactics of the Iraq Insurgency*. Charleston, SC: BookSurge, 2007. A historical analysis of the growth of the anti-American insurgency in Iraq following the 2003 U.S. invasion of that country.

Jessica Stern, *Terror in the Name of God: Why Religious Militants Kill*. New York: HarperCollins, 2003. A leading U.S. expert on terrorism provides a thorough explanation of jihad terrorism and jihad organizations.

David J. Whittaker, *Terrorism: Understanding the Global Threat*. Upper Saddle River, NJ: Longman, 2007. An accessible exploration of the definition, origins, and future of terrorism.

Periodicals

Peter Bergen, "Where You Bin? The Return of Al Qaeda," *The New Republic*, January 29, 2007, p. 16.

Tony Blair, "A Battle for Global Values," *Foreign Affairs*, January–February 2007, Vol. 86, p. 79.

Marvin J. Cetron, "Defeating Terrorism: Is It Possible? Is It Probable?" *The Futurist*, May–June 2007, Vol. 41, p. 18.

Richard A. Clarke, "Ten Years Later," *Atlantic Monthly*, January/February 2005. http://www.theatlantic.com/doc/200501/clarke.

The Economist, "Visions of Osama bin Laden: Al-Qaeda's Leader Returns and Foresees Victory in Iraq," September 13, 2007.

Bruce Hoffman, "The Logic of Suicide Terrorism," *Atlantic Monthly*, June 2003, Vol. 291, Iss. 5, p. 40.

Scott S. Johnson, "The Next Battlefront," *Newsweek*, September 17, 2007. www.msnbc.msn.com/id/20657234/site/newsweek/.

Web Sites

Columbia University Libraries, "The World Trade Center Attack" (www.columbia.edu/cu/lweb/indiv/usgd/wtc.html.) A selective guide to the official government documents related to the terrorist attack on the World Trade Center in New York on September 11, 2001.

Federal Bureau of Investigation (FBI), Counterterrorism (www.fbi. gov/terrorinfo/counterrorism/waronterrorhome.htm.) A federal law enforcement Web site that provides information about terrorism as well as pictures and descriptions of the agency's most wanted terrorists.

Jihad Watch (www.jihadwatch.org.) A private Web site dedicated to bringing public attention to the role that jihad plays in the modern world, and to alert people to the present global conflict being waged by radical Islam.

U.S. Department of Homeland Security (www.dhs.gov.) The home Web site for the U.S. government agency charged with protecting the country from terrorism.

U.S. Department of State, Country Reports on Terrorism 2006 (www.state.gov/s/ct/rls/crt/2006/.) A government site that provides reports on terrorist groups, their umbrella groups, state sponsors of terror, and terrorism activities on a country and regional basis.

U.S. Department of State Counterterrorism Office (www.state.gov/ s/ct/.) A government Web site on counterterrorism that offers an overview of U.S. efforts to combat terrorism, annual reports on global terrorism patterns, and travel alerts.

INDEX

PICTURE CREDITS

Cover Photo: © Carolina K. Smith MD, 2007/Shutterstock.com
AP Images, 17, 22, 39, 41, 43, 46, 51, 57, 59, 63, 64, 67, 75, 79, 88
© Maher Attar/Corbis Sygma, 37
© Bettmann/Corbis, 34
Gale, Cengage Learning, 18, 19, 29, 30
Stephen Jaffe/Getty Images, 7
Abid Katib/Getty Images, 81
Jamal Nasrallah/AFP/Getty Images, 83
© Reuters/Corbis, 8, 26
© Reuters/NewMedia Inc/Corbis, 54
© Ramin Talaie/Corbis, 69
Time & Life Pictures/Getty Images, 15
© Topham/The Image Works, 21
© Peter Turnley/Corbis, 53

ABOUT THE AUTHOR

Debra A. Miller is a writer and lawyer with a passion for current events, history, and public policy. She began her law career in Washington, D.C., where she worked on legislative, policy, and legal matters in government, public interest, and private law firm positions. She now lives with her husband in Encinitas, California. She has written and edited numerous books and anthologies on historical, political, health, and other topics.